Solutions

Pre-Intermediate   Student's Book

Tim Falla, Paul A Davies

OXFORD
UNIVERSITY PRESS

🎧 Listening (1.01 = disk 1, track 1 / 2.01 = disk 2, track 1)

1 The real you

THIS UNIT INCLUDES ●●●●●
Vocabulary • personality adjectives • negative prefixes: *un-*, *im-* / *in-* and *dis-*
• hobbies and interests • time phrases
Grammar • present simple and continuous • verbs not used in continuous tenses
• verb + infinitive or *-ing* form
Speaking • talking about personality • expressing likes and dislikes
Writing • a personal profile

A VOCABULARY AND LISTENING
Personalities

I can describe someone's personality.

1 Look at the photos. Do you know the characters? Is each person:
- kind or unkind?
- funny or serious?
- lazy or hard-working?
- generous or mean?

> I think Trinity is serious.

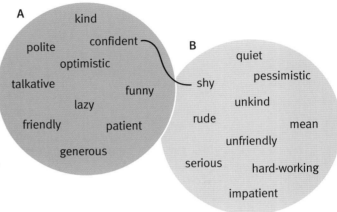
Trinity

Blofeld

Garfield

Yoda

Cruella de Vil

2 Match the personality adjectives in A with their opposites in B.

Personality adjectives

A
kind
polite   confident
optimistic
talkative
funny
lazy
friendly   patient
generous

B
quiet
shy   pessimistic
unkind
rude   mean
unfriendly
serious   hard-working
impatient

3 🎧 1.01 Listen, repeat and check.

●●●● Vocabulary Builder (part 1): page 124

4 🎧 1.02 Listen to the dialogues and match an adjective in the box with each person in the table. You will not need all the words.

generous	impatient	lazy	pessimistic	rude	shy

1 Martin	
2 Julie	
3 Terry	
4 Emma	

5 Make notes about three friends or relatives. What personality adjectives can you use to describe them? Give reasons.

Tom (brother) – lazy – doesn't help around the house
Susan (sister) ...

6 **SPEAKING** Tell the class about your friends or relatives.

> My brother, Tom, is very lazy. He never does any work around the house. My sister, Susan, is ...

●●●● Vocabulary Builder (part 2): page 124

Present simple and continuous

I can say what I usually do and what I'm doing now.

1 Look at the picture. What are the people doing? Use the verbs in the box.

| Useful verbs | carry | chat | dance | drink | eat | hold |
| laugh | listen | relax | sit | smile | stand | text |

> A woman is dancing. She's smiling.

2 Read the text messages. What does Ed think of the wedding?

Cath
Hi Ed. Are you having a good time?

Ed
No, I'm not. I don't know many people here. I'm not talking to anyone. And I'm wearing a stupid tie!

Cath
A tie?! You never wear ties. Send me a photo! I need a laugh. By the way, I'm going to my cousin's wedding next weekend.

Ed
Do you like weddings? They're so boring. My grandad always falls asleep. He's got the right idea!

3 Look at the table. Underline examples of the present simple and present continuous in the text messages.

Present simple	
affirmative	She always wears jeans.
negative	He doesn't like impatient people.
interrogative	Do you want a drink?
Present continuous	
affirmative	She's sending a text message.
negative	They aren't wearing any shoes.
interrogative	Is he playing the keyboard?

4 Complete the rules in the *Learn this!* box with the correct tense.

LEARN THIS!
1 We use the _____ for something that always or regularly happens .
2 We use the _____ for something that is happening now.
3 We use the _____ for a fact that is always true.
4 We use the _____ for arrangements in the future.
5 We don't use the _____ with certain verbs, e.g. *believe, hate, like, love, need, know, prefer, want.*

●○●● Grammar Builder (1B): page 104

5 Complete the dialogue with the present simple or present continuous form of the verbs in brackets.

Naomi Hello. [1]_____ (you/enjoy) the music?
Ed Not really. I [2]_____ (prefer) hip hop. This band is terrible.
Naomi It's my dad's band.
Ed Oh, right. Actually, they [3]_____ (not play) badly now. Lots of people [4]_____ (dance). Which one is your dad?
Naomi He [5]_____ (play) the guitar.
Ed He's great! Anyway, I [6]_____ (not know) your name.
Naomi I'm Naomi.
Ed I'm Ed. Pleased to meet you.
Naomi Hey, I [7]_____ (like) your suit. It's cool.
Ed Really?
Naomi Yes. [8]_____ (you/wear) it often?
Ed Er ... yes. I [9]_____ (wear) it most weekends. Actually, [10]_____ (you/do) anything next weekend?
Naomi Yes. I [11]_____ (visit) my boyfriend at university.
Ed Oh, right.

6 🎧 1.03 Listen and check.

7 SPEAKING Work in pairs. Look at the table. Make two true sentences for each verb, using the present simple and present continuous, and the nouns and time phrases.

Verbs	Nouns	Time phrases
go	my homework	after school
speak	jeans	every day
wear	English	at the moment
do	computer games	today
play	to town	next week
	to school	at weekends
	this exercise	this weekend

> I don't go to school at weekends.

> I'm going to town after school.

1C CULTURE Free time

I can talk about hobbies and interests.

1 Look at the photos. What are the teenagers doing? Which of the activities do you do?

2 Read the text quickly. What do the numbers refer to?

85   1,152 million   75

Teenage leisure in the UK

Computer games and TV

In the UK today, fewer and fewer teenagers are playing games outside with their friends; 85% prefer playing computer games on their own. In fact, playing computer games is one of the most popular leisure activities in the UK. In 2003, British shoppers spent £1,152 million on computer games! In general, boys are more interested in computers than girls.

Teenagers also love watching TV. Watching TV is more popular with boys and girls in the UK than in most other European countries. In the UK, the TV is often on all day, and teenagers watch it before and after school. More than half of children have a television in their bedroom, and about a third also have a video recorder.

Sport and exercise

A lot of people are worried that today's British teenagers don't get enough exercise. Today, less than half of teenagers play team sports, compared to more than 75% in the 1970s. More than 80% of teenagers in the UK now prefer watching sport on TV to actually playing it. More than half of teenagers agree that young people are getting 'fatter, lazier and more addicted to computer games.' They want to play sports, they say, but a lot of local parks and sports centres are closing. New gyms are opening, but they're too expensive for most teenagers.

Essential facts

Average time teenagers in the UK spend playing sport:
• 15–25 minutes per day for girls
• 40–55 minutes per day for boys

Average time teenagers in the UK spend watching TV:
• 2.5 hours a day

3 Read the text again and answer the questions.

1 In the UK, are boys or girls more interested in computers?
2 Do teenagers in the UK watch more or less TV than teenagers in other European countries?
3 How many children in the UK have a video recorder in their bedroom?
4 How many teenagers in the UK today play team sports?
5 Why don't teenagers go to new gyms?
6 How long do teenagers spend watching TV on average in the UK?

4 🎧 1.04 Listen to four conversations about free-time activities. Match the teenagers with their hobbies.

1	Duncan	a	riding a BMX bike
2	Shama	b	computer games
3	Martin	c	chess
4	Karen	d	listening to music

5 Complete the sentences with the names of the teenagers from exercise 4. Which sentences are also true for you?

1 _____ has a lot of different hobbies and interests.
2 _____ doesn't get very much physical exercise.
3 _____ has a hobby that might become a profession.
4 _____ is very keen on physical exercise.
5 _____ sometimes goes dancing in clubs.
6 _____ doesn't watch TV but watches films.
7 _____ does aerobics.
8 _____ spends a lot of time surfing the Internet.

6 🎧 1.04 Listen again and check.

7 🎧 1.05 **PRONUNCIATION** Listen and repeat the questions from the interviews. Copy the intonation.

1 What do you do in your free time?
2 How much time do you spend watching TV?
3 Have you got any other hobbies?
4 Do you play computer games on your own or with friends?
5 What about sport and exercise?
6 What kind of music do you listen to?
7 What else do you like doing?
8 Do you watch a lot of TV?

8 **SPEAKING** Interview your partner about his or her free-time activities. Use questions from exercise 7 and your own ideas.

1 **SPEAKING** Work in pairs. Ask and answer the questions. Make a note of your answers.

Are you FEARLESS or PHOBIC?

1 You want to have a shower but there's a big spider. Do you
 a avoid having a shower?
 b have a shower anyway?

2 You're at a party where there are a lot of people you don't know. Do you
 a decide to leave?
 b spend time making new friends?

3 Travelling by plane is very safe, but what is your opinion of flying?
 a I can't help feeling nervous.
 b I don't mind flying at all.

4 Somebody offers to give you a free ticket to a big rock concert. Do you
 a say no because you can't stand being in a very large crowd of people?
 b accept the ticket?

5 You're in a lift when it gets stuck. Do you
 a feel scared because you imagine being in the lift for hours?
 b wait patiently and hope to be free soon?

6 A friend suggests doing a bungee jump. Do you
 a refuse to do it because you're afraid of heights?
 b agree to do it?

2 Look at your answers and count the *a*s and *b*s. Are you fearless (mostly *b*s) or phobic (mostly *a*s)?

3 Study the information in the *Learn this!* box. Underline all the verbs in the questionnaire that are followed by the infinitive or *-ing* form of another verb.

> **LEARN THIS!**
>
> **1** Some verbs are followed by the infinitive of another verb.
> *I'm pretending to be ill.*
>
> **2** Some verbs are followed by the *-ing* form of another verb.
> *I don't fancy going out tonight.*

4 Complete the table with the verbs that you underlined in the questionnaire.

Verb + infinitive	Verb + *-ing* form
pretend	fancy

●○●●● Grammar Builder (1D): page 104

5 Complete the sentences with the infinitive or *-ing* form of the verbs in the box.

be	chat	feel	pass	help	pay	study	wait

1 My dad is really kind. He always offers _____ people.
2 I'm quite optimistic. I usually expect _____ my exams.
3 My friend Sarah is really impatient. She can't stand _____ .
4 Sammy is really generous. He always offers _____ .
5 Jane is very hard-working. She doesn't mind _____ for hours.
6 I'm very ambitious. I often imagine _____ rich and famous.
7 Mark is so talkative! He keeps _____ even when nobody is listening!
8 My sister is so shy. She can't help _____ nervous when a boy talks to her.

6 Complete the sentences with an infinitive or *-ing* form and true information about yourself.

1 I usually avoid …
2 I really can't stand …
3 I don't mind …
4 I spend a lot of time …
5 I really want …
6 I sometimes pretend …

7 **SPEAKING** Tell the class your sentences. Does anybody have the same answers?

I can understand an article and a song about youth culture.

1 Describe the people in the photos. Do young people dress like this in your country?

2 Read the text. Do you think people are right or wrong to ban hoodies?

Do goodies wear hoodies?

There are lots of clothes shops in the Bluewater Shopping Centre in the south of England, so it's easy to find fashionable hooded tops for sale there. However, you can't wear a hooded top while you're looking, because they're banned . The shopping centre
5 believes that teenagers who wear hooded tops often use them to hide their faces while they're behaving badly. That's why the new rule bans people wearing 'hoodies' (hooded tops) from the shopping centre. Baseball caps are also banned. And the managers of the shopping centre say that their new rules are working. More
10 people are shopping there, and trouble-makers are staying away.

The Bluewater Shopping Centre is not the only place in the UK where certain clothes are banned. Students at Maesteg Comprehensive School in Wales are not allowed to wear hooded tops because the head teacher believes that they cause bad
15 behaviour. If children wear hooded tops to school, the teachers take them away, and don't give them back until the end of term. Most of the parents agree with this new rule.

However, many people, especially young people, believe that these rules are silly and unfair. They say that baseball caps and
20 hooded tops are an important part of teenage fashion, and it's impossible to judge a person's personality from the clothes they wear. The head teacher of Coombeshead College in the south of England agrees. In fact, hooded tops are now part of the school uniform at Coombeshead College.

25 Many adults believe that young people's behaviour is getting worse. One politician, Lord Ashley, said, 'Children are ten times worse than in the past.' However, he said that in 1823! The generation gap is nothing new.

3 Choose the best answers.

1 At the Bluewater Shopping Centre
  a there aren't any fashionable clothes.
  b hooded tops and baseball caps are banned.
  c only hooded tops are banned.
  d teenagers are banned.

2 The result of the ban is
  a clothes shops are closing.
  b teenagers are hiding their faces.
  c there are more teenagers in the shops.
  d there are more customers in the shops.

3 Students at Maesteg Comprehensive School
  a are not allowed to wear hooded tops.
  b cannot shop at the Bluewater Shopping Centre.
  c all support the new rule.
  d all behave very badly.

4 The head teacher of Coombeshead College doesn't believe that
  a young people behave well.
  b hooded tops are fashionable.
  c you can judge a person by their clothes.
  d school uniform is a good idea.

5 Why did the writer of the article include Lord Ashley's statement?
  a To show that adults always think children behave badly.
  b To show that children always behave badly.
  c To show that children behaved well in 1823.
  d To show that adults are the same as children.

4 Match the highlighted words and phrases in the text with the correct definitions below.

1 form an opinion of _____
2 have the same opinion _____
3 in a shop, ready for people to buy _____
4 people who behave badly _____
5 doing and saying things in a certain way _____
6 something you are not allowed to do _____
7 stupid; not sensible _____
8 the difference in opinions between young people and older people _____

5 🎧 1.06 Listen to *Sk8er Boi* by Avril Lavigne. Complete the song with the words in the box.

baggy	earth	ends	girl	guitar	home	inside
pretty	punk	show	skater	skater	skater	song
tickets	TV					

6 Choose the best summary of the lyrics.

a A boy liked you, but you didn't want him because of his clothes. Now he's a star, but you can't change your mind because I'm with him now!
b You went to a concert with your friends. You liked the guitarist, but he didn't talk to you because he was a star.
c You saw a guitarist on MTV and fell in love. Now you always go to his concerts with your friends, but they don't like the music.

7 SPEAKING Work in pairs. What do you think is the message of the song?

a Don't fall in love with rock stars.
b Don't always do what your friends tell you.
c Always tell your friends how you feel.
d Don't listen to pop music.

> I think it's *a* because rock stars are unfriendly and rude.

> I disagree. I think it's ...

Sk8er Boi

He was a boy, she was a [1]_____
Can I make it any more obvious?
He was a [2]_____ , she did ballet
What more can I say?
He wanted her
She'd never tell secretly she wanted him as well
But all of her friends stuck up their nose
They had a problem with his [3]_____ clothes

He was a [4]_____ boy
She said see you later boy
He wasn't good enough for her
She had a [5]_____ face
But her head was up in space
She needed to come back down to [6]_____

Five years from now she sits at [7]_____
Feeding the baby she's all alone
She turns on [8]_____, guess who she sees
Skater boy rockin' up MTV
She calls up her friends
They already know
And they've all got [9]_____ to see his show
She tags along, stands in the crowd
Looks up at the man that she turned down

He was a [10]_____ boy
She said see you later boy
He wasn't good enough for her
Now he's a superstar
Slamming on his [11]_____
Does your pretty face see what he's worth?

Sorry girl but you missed out
Well tough luck that boy's mine now
We are more than just good friends
This is how the story [12]_____
Too bad that you couldn't see,
See the man that boy could be
There is more than meets the eye
I see the soul that is [13]_____

He's just a boy and I'm just a girl
Can I make it any more obvious?
We are in love. Haven't you heard
How we rock each other's world?

I'm with the [14]_____ boy
I said see you later boy
I'll be backstage after the [15]_____
I'll be at the studio
Singing the [16]_____ we wrote
About a girl you used to know

Glossary
rockin' up MTV = playing rock music on MTV

tags along = goes with them

slamming on his guitar = playing the guitar very loudly

we rock each other's world = we're in love

Giving an opinion

I can express my likes and dislikes.

Alice What do you like doing in your free time?
Jack I enjoy going to the cinema.
Alice Me too. But I'd rather watch TV.
Jack Really? I often watch TV during the week, but at the weekend, I prefer going to the cinema.
Alice What else do you like doing?
Jack I love surfing the Internet.
Alice Do you? I can't stand surfing the Internet.
Jack And I quite like playing tennis, too.
Alice So do I. Do you fancy playing tennis this weekend?
Jack Sure! Good idea.

1 🎧 **1.07** Read and listen to the dialogue. Underline phrases that mean:

1 I really like …
2 I really don't like …
3 I prefer …
4 Would you like to …?

2 SPEAKING Work in pairs. Practise reading the dialogue, changing the words in blue. Use phrases from the box and your own ideas.

Hobbies and interests chatting online dancing doing sport drawing going out with friends listening to music reading shopping taking photos playing chess playing computer games

Exam tip

Go to the *Functions Bank* in the Workbook for more phrases and expressions you can use in a conversation.

3 🎧 **1.08** Listen to four conversations. Complete the table with phrases a–d.

a listening to music – singers
b eating out – kinds of food
c shopping – shops
d ~~watching sport – sports~~

	both like …	but prefer different …
1 Fred and Chloe	watching sport	sports
2 Simon and Tara		
3 Kevin and Lucy		
4 John and Pam		

4 🎧 **1.08** Listen again. Answer the questions.

1 What does Chloe prefer?
2 What does Simon hate?
3 Who does Lucy like?
4 What does John love?

5 🎧 **1.09** PRONUNCIATION Study the speaking tip. Listen and repeat, copying the intonation of the phrases.

Speaking tip

In a conversation, react to what the other person says using phrases such as:
Do you? Really? Me too! So do I! That's interesting!

6 Work in pairs. Take turns to say the sentences and react to them.

I like going out with friends.
Me too!

1 I like going out with friends.
2 I quite like playing computer games.
3 I often go to the cinema on Friday evenings.
4 I can't stand reading newspapers.
5 I prefer watching football on TV to playing it.

7 SPEAKING Work in pairs. Prepare a dialogue following the chart below. Make notes.

A
Ask B what he/she likes doing.

B
Answer the question.

React to B's answer. Then say you prefer another activity.

React to A. Say you like that activity too.

Suggest doing the activity.

Agree.

8 SPEAKING Act out your dialogue to the class.

A personal profile

I can write a personal profile for an Internet chatroom.

1 Read the writing task and the two personal profiles. Have the writers:

1 included all the information?
2 written the correct number of words?

Writing task

Write a personal profile of 80–100 words for an Internet chatroom. Call your profile 'The real me'. Include:

• an introduction with your name, hometown, age and brief information about your school and family
• information about hobbies, interests and sports
• a description of your personality

The real me **by Martin**

My name is Martin and I'm from London. I'm 16 years old and I'm in year 11 at Parkfield School.

I've got lots of hobbies and interests. I love playing chess and computer games with my brother. I also do a lot of sport – I particularly enjoy swimming and karate. I'm also interested in photography.

I'm quite an ambitious person. I want to go to university and then get a job in web design. I think I'm quite hard-working, too. I've probably got a few faults. I think I'm slightly impatient and maybe a little intolerant too.

The real me **by Sarah**

My name is Sarah. I'm 17 and I go to Greenhill School. I'm in year 12. I live with my parents and my brother Jake.

My hobbies are fashion and listening to music. I'm not very keen on sport, but I play volleyball at school.

I'm not at all a shy person. I'm quite confident and I prefer talking to other confident people. I think I'm kind and very loyal to my friends.

---

2 Answer the questions for each person.

1 How old are they?
2 What year are they in at school?
3 Which sports do they like?
4 What other hobbies and interests do they have?
5 What personality adjectives do they use to describe themselves?

3 Read the writing tip. Underline all the modifying adverbs in the personal profiles. Translate them.

Writing tip: using modifying adverbs

We use modifying adverbs to make the meaning of adjectives stronger or weaker.
a little   not at all   quite   really   slightly   very

4 Look at the modifying adverbs in the personal profiles. Underline the correct words in the rules below.

1 Modifying adverbs usually go **before** / **after** the adjective.
2 The modifying adverbs *quite* and *not at all* go **before** / **after** *a/an* when there is a noun.

5 Rewrite the sentences to include the modifying adverb in brackets.

1 I'm pessimistic. (slightly)
2 My best friend is confident. (really)
3 He's an impatient person. (not at all)
4 I'm a student at a big school. (quite)
5 I find English difficult. (quite)
6 I'm sometimes shy. (a bit)

6 Look again at the writing task in exercise 1. Make notes about yourself. Organise your ideas into three sections.

7 Write your personal profile.

8 Check that you have completed the writing task correctly by ticking the boxes.

☐ name
☐ age
☐ town/village
☐ school
☐ family
☐ hobbies & interests
☐ sports
☐ personality
☐ 80–100 words

1 `Get ready to SPEAK` **Match 1–5 with a–e to make true sentences about the photo.**

1 The boy on the left
2 The girl on the right
3 The boy in the background
4 The girl in the middle
5 The group of people in the foreground

a is wearing a white T-shirt.
b are smiling at each other.
c is wearing a yellow T-shirt.
d has long, dark hair.
e has books in her left hand.

2 🎧 1.10 **Listen to Peter describing the photo. Tick the phrases he uses.**

☐ 1 **I think that** they are about 14 or 15 years old.
☐ 2 **Personally, I think** they are over 15 years old.
☐ 3 **In my opinion** they are studying something.
☐ 4 **Perhaps** they are on a language course in Britain.
☐ 5 **I don't think** they are studying in the summer holidays.
☐ 6 **In my view** they are friends because they look very relaxed.
☐ 7 **I'm not sure** why they are so happy.

3 **Do you agree or disagree with Peter's opinions? Use the language for expressing opinions (in bold in exercise 2) to help you answer.**
For example: *Perhaps they are on a study trip in the USA.*

4 **Do the Speaking exam task.**

SPEAKING exam task

Answer the questions about the photo. Give reasons for your opinions.

1 Where are the people in the photo?
2 What are they doing?
3 Why do you think they are so happy?
4 What makes you happy in everyday life and why?

5 🎧 1.11 **Do the Listening exam task.**

LISTENING exam task

Listen to six people introducing themselves. Complete the table.

	Age	Country	Hobbies
Ralf			
Kate			
Marie			
Marco			
Liam			
Laurent			

6 **Work in pairs. Choose two people from exercise 1 and answer the questions.**

1 How old are they?
2 Where are they from?
3 What are their hobbies?

7 **Do the Use of English exam task.**

USE OF ENGLISH exam task

Complete the text with the correct form of the words given.

My best friend is called Sarah. She's in the same class as me at school. We always sit next to each other. She's very ¹_____ (FRIEND) and she always helps me with my homework. She's also very ²_____ (TALK) – the teachers sometimes tell her off – but she's always telling ³_____ (FUN) jokes. My one criticism of her is that she's a bit ⁴_____ (PATIENT). We spend a lot of time together because we share the same hobbies – we're both ⁵_____ (INTEREST) in music and fashion, and we both love playing volleyball.

8 **What part of speech are the missing words in exercise 7?**

Tip

In the exam, read the text and, for each gap, identify the part of speech that is missing. (In exercise 7, the missing words are all adjectives, but in the exam there will be a variety of missing parts of speech.)

Get ready for your EXAM 2

1 `Get ready to READ` Work in pairs. Who do you talk to about your feelings?

- your friends
- your brother or sister
- your parents
- your teacher

2 Do the Reading exam task.

READING exam task

- Read the text and match headings A–D with paragraphs 1–3. There is one extra heading that you don't need.
- Mark the sentences T (*true*), F (*false*) or NK (*not known*).

Sometimes the hardest thing about feelings is sharing them with others. But sharing your feelings helps you feel better and also helps you to get closer to people who are important to you.

1 You can't tell your friends what's in your backpack if you don't know what's in there yourself. Feelings are the same. Before you can share them with anyone, you have to understand what feelings you have. Making a list of your feelings can help. You can do this in your head or by writing it out on a piece of paper. It's sometimes difficult to define a feeling and its cause. In this case, it might help to remember how you felt on a specific occasion, for example, 'I was upset when my friends went to the cinema without me.'

2 Keeping your feelings to yourself can make you feel worse. If you talk to someone who cares for you, like your parents, you will almost always start to feel better. It doesn't mean your problems will magically disappear, but at least someone else knows what the problem is and can help you find solutions. If you don't want to talk to your parents, then try talking to a relative or a counsellor at school. Maybe they can help you find a way to talk to your parents about your problems.

3 Once you know who you can talk to, choose a time and place to talk. If you think you'll have trouble saying what you're thinking, write it down on a piece of paper. If the person doesn't understand what you mean, try giving an example of what's concerning you. Some people are more private than others and feel more shy about sharing their feelings. You don't have to share every feeling you have, but it is important to share feelings when you need help.

A How to talk about your feelings
B Why do we have feelings?
C Why is it better to talk about your feelings?
D Focusing on your feelings

1 The text is directed at adults. ☐
2 Sharing your feelings improves your relationship with people that are close to you. ☐
3 You don't need to understand your feelings before sharing them with others. ☐
4 You should never talk about your feelings with someone you don't know. ☐
5 It isn't necessary to express every emotion. ☐

3 `SPEAKING` Work in pairs. What advice does the article give you about sharing your feelings?

4 Choose the correct tense, present simple or present continuous.

1 I **feel / 'm feeling** happy when I'm at home with my family.
2 I **never share / 'm never sharing** my feelings with my friends.
3 John is worried because he **doesn't think / isn't thinking** that he'll pass his exams.
4 'Why **do you laugh / are you laughing**?' 'Because Joe told a funny joke.'
5 What **do you wear / are you wearing** to Tom's party this evening?
6 Jane **loves / is loving** going out with her friends.
7 Sue **cries / is crying** because her brother is in hospital.
8 **Do you remember / Are you remembering** how you felt when you won the football match?

5 🎧 1.12 Listen to Kati and David discussing the things that are important to them. Tick the things they think are important.

	Kati	David
friends	☐	☐
family	☐	☐
money	☐	☐
sport	☐	☐
girlfriend/boyfriend	☐	☐
school	☐	☐

6 🎧 1.12 Complete the sentences with the words in the box. Then listen again and check.

as	both	more	most	second	than

1 I think the _____ important thing is spending time with my friends.
2 Well, they're _____ very important.
3 I think that spending time with my friends is _____ important.
4 It certainly isn't as important _____ being good at sport.
5 Is having a girlfriend more important _____ being good at sport?
6 Personally, I think the _____ most important thing is doing well at school.

7 Do the Speaking exam task.

SPEAKING exam task

Choose two things from the list that make you happy. Give reasons for your opinions.

1 spending time with your friends
2 doing well at school
3 having lots of money
4 having a boyfriend/girlfriend
5 being good at sport
6 spending time with your family

2 Winning and losing

THIS UNIT INCLUDES ●●●●●
Vocabulary • sports • *play/go/do* + sport • collocations: sports and games
• free-time activities
Grammar • past simple • contrast: past simple and past continuous
Speaking • talking about favourite sports • talking about the past • narrating a story
Writing • a magazine article

A VOCABULARY AND LISTENING
A question of sport

I can talk about sports I like.

1 SPEAKING **Work in pairs. Ask and answer the questions. Then check your scores.**

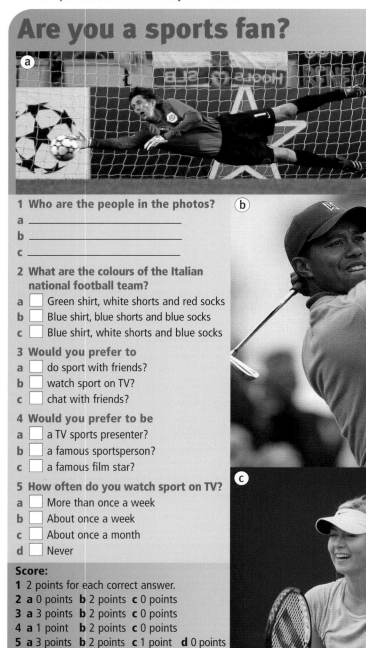

Are you a sports fan?

1 Who are the people in the photos?
a _____
b _____
c _____

2 What are the colours of the Italian national football team?
a ☐ Green shirt, white shorts and red socks
b ☐ Blue shirt, blue shorts and blue socks
c ☐ Blue shirt, white shorts and blue socks

3 Would you prefer to
a ☐ do sport with friends?
b ☐ watch sport on TV?
c ☐ chat with friends?

4 Would you prefer to be
a ☐ a TV sports presenter?
b ☐ a famous sportsperson?
c ☐ a famous film star?

5 How often do you watch sport on TV?
a ☐ More than once a week
b ☐ About once a week
c ☐ About once a month
d ☐ Never

Score:
1 2 points for each correct answer.
2 a 0 points **b** 2 points **c** 0 points
3 a 3 points **b** 2 points **c** 0 points
4 a 1 point **b** 2 points **c** 0 points
5 a 3 points **b** 2 points **c** 1 point **d** 0 points

13–16 points You are sports mad!
6–12 points You like sport but there are more important things in life.
0–5 points You aren't really interested in sport.

2 Match the words in the box with the pictures.

Sports athletics badminton baseball basketball
cycling football golf gymnastics ice hockey judo
karate rugby surfing swimming table tennis
tennis volleyball weightlifting

3 🎧 1.13 Listen, repeat and check.

4 Read the information in the *Look out!* box. Match the other sports from exercise 2 to the three verbs.

Look out!
We normally use
play with team sports and ball sports.
play badminton
go with sports that end in -*ing*.
go cycling
do with other sports.
do athletics

●●●● **Vocabulary Builder (part 1): page 125**

5 🎧 1.14 Listen to eight short sports commentaries. Identify the sports.

6 SPEAKING **Work in pairs. Ask and answer the questions. Make notes of your partner's answers.**
1 What sports do you enjoy doing?
2 When do you do them?
3 Where do you do them?
4 What sports do you enjoy watching on TV?
5 Who/What are your favourite players/teams?

7 SPEAKING **Tell the class about your partner.**

Becky enjoys doing athletics and going swimming. She …

●●●● **Vocabulary Builder (part 2): page 125**

2B GRAMMAR
Past simple

I can describe past events.

1 Read the text and choose the best answers.

1 **One team** / **Both teams** cheated.

2 **Arsenal** / **Dynamo Moscow** won the match.

On 21 November 1945, Arsenal played Dynamo Moscow in London. It was very foggy that day. In the first half, the referee sent off an Arsenal player, but he came back on a few minutes later. The referee didn't notice because of the fog! Dynamo Moscow cheated too. At one moment in the second half, fifteen Moscow players were on the pitch at the same time! How did the match finish? Dynamo Moscow 4, Arsenal 3.

2 Underline the following past simple forms in the text.

1 two affirmative regular verbs

2 two forms of *be* (singular and plural)

3 two affirmative irregular verbs

4 a negative form and an interrogative form

3 Complete the box with the correct past simple form of *play*, *go* or *do*.

Past simple
affirmative
I _____ basketball at the gym yesterday.
We _____ surfing last Saturday.
negative
My sister _____ gymnastics until she was seven.
interrogative
_____ they _____ swimming in the sea?

> **Look out!**
>
> We don't use *did* or *didn't* with the past simple negative and interrogative form of *be*.
> *Were you at the match? It wasn't very exciting.*

4 🎧 1.15 **PRONUNCIATION** Listen and repeat the past simple forms. How is the *-ed* ending pronounced? Write the correct sound next to each verb: /d/ /t/ or /ɪd/.

1 played <u>d</u>

2 cheated ___

3 finished ___

4 kicked ___

5 scored ___

6 competed ___

7 passed ___

8 watched ___

⦁⦁⦁●●● Grammar Builder (2B): page 106

At the Sydney Olympics in 2000, the biggest cheer from the spectators at the swimming pool [1] _____ (come) when Eric Moussambani [2] _____ (finish) the 100 metres freestyle. Eric [3] _____ (not win) the event. In fact, his time [4] _____ (be) 1 minute 53 seconds, the slowest time in Olympic history. Eric, from Equatorial Guinea in Africa, only [5] _____ (learn) to swim eight months before he [6] _____ (compete) in the Olympics.

In a tennis match in 1998 between Pete Sampras and Patrick Rafter, Rafter [7] _____ (become) angry with himself when he [8] _____ (miss) an easy shot. He [9] _____ (give) his racket to Chad Little, one of the ball boys, and [10] _____ (shout): 'You play!' Chad [11] _____ (not know) what to do, so he [12] _____ (get) ready to play the next point against Sampras. More than 10,000 spectators [13] _____ (cheer).

5 Complete the stories above using the past simple form of the verbs in brackets.

6 🎧 1.16 Listen and check.

7 Complete the questions about the stories.

1 _____ the 100 metres freestyle?
No, he didn't. He finished last.

2 What _____ time?
1 minute 53 seconds.

3 When _____ to swim?
Eight months before the Olympics.

4 Why _____ angry?
Because he missed an easy shot.

5 What _____ to Chad Little?
His racket.

6 What _____ to Chad Little?
'You play!'

8 Write three sentences about what happened last weekend, two true and one false.

My uncle Stan visited us and we went to a football match.

9 **SPEAKING** Tell the class your sentences. The class votes on which sentence they think is false.

2C CULTURE
On the river
I can understand information about a sporting event.

1 Describe the photo using words from the box. Check the meanings in your dictionary.

Nouns	bank (of a river) buildings oar river rowers boat spectators
Verbs	cheer lead row wave

2 Read the text and answer the questions.

1 When does the race take place?
2 Where does the race take place?
3 Who competes in the race?

The Boat Race

The Boat Race takes place in London every year in the spring. It is a race between two teams – one from Oxford University and the other from Cambridge University. Each team has eight rowers and a 'cox', the person who shouts instructions to the rowers and steers the boat. The rowers are usually very big and strong (often about 200 centimetres tall), but the cox is usually small and light so that the boat doesn't have to carry much extra weight.

The teams spend months preparing for the race. They begin training in September. Then, in December, there are practice races – but not between Oxford and Cambridge. Teams from the same university compete in practice races so that they can choose the best rowers for the 'big' race in the spring.

The race takes place along the river Thames, in west London. The course is 6,779 metres from start to finish. It is an extremely popular event. Every year, about 250,000 spectators watch the race from the banks of the river, and about half a billion people around the world watch it on TV.

3 Answer the questions.

1 How many rowers are there in a team?
2 Why is the cox usually small?
3 When do the teams begin training?
4 What happens in December?
5 How long is the race?
6 How many people watch the race from the banks?

4 🎧 1.17 Listen to the radio programme about the history of the Boat Race. Number the events in the order you hear about them.

a dead heat
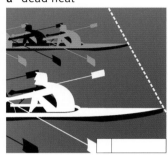

b female cox

c TV broadcast

d crashed
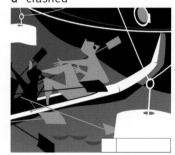

e fastest time
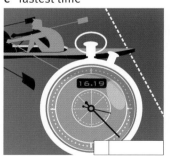

f both sank

5 🎧 1.17 Listen again and write the correct year next to each picture.

6 SPEAKING Work in pairs. Ask and answer questions about the history of the Boat Race.

What happened in 1912?

Both boats sank.

Who won in …?

2D **GRAMMAR**
Past simple and continuous
I can tell a short story using past tenses.

1 🎧 **1.18 Read and listen. Are the sentences true or false?**

1 Lauda had an accident on 1 August 1976.
2 It was raining that day.
3 Guy Edwards caused the accident.

On 1 August 1976, Niki Lauda was racing in the German Grand Prix when he had a terrible accident. The weather was bad – it was raining. While Lauda was going round a corner, he suddenly lost control of his Ferrari. The car crashed and caught fire. Another driver, Guy Edwards, was coming towards the corner when he saw Lauda inside the burning car. He stopped and pulled Lauda out.

2 **Look at the past continuous forms in the text. Complete the table with the correct form of the verb *be*.**

Past continuous
affirmative
I _____ sleeping. We _____ reading.
negative
It _____ raining. They _____ listening.
interrogative
_____ you playing? What _____ he doing?

3 **Study the information in the *Learn this!* box. Underline one example of each use in the text in exercise 1.**

LEARN THIS!

1 We use the **past continuous** to describe a scene in the past.
The sun was shining. Birds were singing.

2 We use the **past simple** for a sequence of actions or events that happened one after the other.
I stood up, walked to the door and left the room.

3 We use the **past continuous** and the **past simple** together when we describe a sudden action or event that interrupted a longer action or event.
While I was walking to school, my phone rang.
        [longer action]   [interruption]

●●●●● Grammar Builder (2D): page 106

4 **Complete the text with the past simple or past continuous form of the verbs in brackets.**

It was 17 March 1984. Thousands of people ¹_____ (stand) on the banks of the river Thames in London. They ²_____ (wait) for the start of the annual Oxford and Cambridge Boat Race. But while the Cambridge boat ³_____ (go) under a bridge, it ⁴_____ (hit) another boat. Soon, it was clear that the boat ⁵_____ (sink), so they ⁶_____ (row) to the bank. The race ⁷_____ (take place) the next day – and Cambridge ⁸_____ (lose).

5 **SPEAKING** **Work in pairs. Look at the cartoon story and answer the questions. Use the words in brackets to help you.**

1 What was the weather like? (the sun/shine, warm)
   What was the girl doing? (sit/on a bench, watch/baseball match)
2 What did the player do? (hit the ball)
   What did the dog do? (run onto the pitch)
3 What did the dog do next? (catch the ball)
   What happened to the player? (fall over)
4 What did the girl do? (take the dog off the pitch)
   What were the spectators doing? (laugh and cheer)

6 **SPEAKING** **Work in pairs. Look at the cartoon story for one more minute. Close your books and tell the story to your partner. Use the past simple and past continuous.**

The sun was shining. It was a lovely warm day. A girl was sitting …

1 **Describe** the photos. What do you think happened to the surfer?

Exam tip

Look at the photo and the title and try to guess what the text is about.

2 **Read** the first two paragraphs and check your answers.

3 **Read** the text. Put the events in the correct order.

- ☐ The shark swam away.
- ☐ Ten weeks later she took part in a surfing competition.
- ☐ She started to swim back to the beach.
- ☐ She decided to go surfing with some friends.
- ☐ Her friends saw the blood and came to help her.
- ☐ While she was waiting for a wave, a shark attacked her.

Surfing superstar!

On the morning of 31 October 2003 Bethany Hamilton decided to go surfing with some friends in Hawaii. The sky was clear, the sun was shining and it was a perfect day for surfing on the big waves near the island of Kauai.

5 The 13-year-old surfing star was lying on her surfboard about 300 metres from the beach. She was waiting for the next big wave, and her arms were hanging in the clear, blue water. Suddenly a five-metre tiger shark bit her left arm and shook her backwards and forwards. Bethany held onto her board and
10 the shark eventually swam away – but it took her arm with it. It also took a huge piece of her board. Luckily it attacked only once. It happened so fast that Bethany didn't even scream .

Bethany was one of the best teenage surfers in the world, and was planning to become a professional surfer . Immediately
15 after the attack, she thought: 'I need to get back to the beach' and 'Will I lose my sponsors ?' Her friends didn't see the attack, and as Bethany started swimming back to the beach with one arm, they thought at first that she was joking . Then they saw the blood and quickly came to help.

20 The really incredible thing about Bethany is that only ten weeks later she was surfing again in a competition. Less than a year after the accident she won first place in a surfing competition in Hawaii. Before the accident a lot of professional surfers thought that Bethany was going to be the women's
25 world champion . Very few of them have changed their opinion.

4 Are the sentences true or false? Correct the false sentences.

1 It was raining on the morning Bethany went surfing.
2 She was lying on her board when the shark attacked.
3 The shark attacked her again a few minutes later.
4 Bethany screamed while the shark was biting her arm.
5 Immediately after the attack, she was worried about her sponsors.
6 Bethany didn't surf again until a year later.
7 A lot of professional surfers still think Bethany can be a champion surfer.

5 Find the past simple form of the verbs in the text.

1 bite (line 8)
2 shake (line 8)
3 hold (line 9)
4 take (line 10)
5 think (line 15)
6 see (line 19)
7 come (line 19)
8 win (line 22)

6 Match the highlighted words in the text with the definitions.

1 behaving in a funny way
2 amazing; unbelievable
3 companies that give money to sports people
4 shout in a very high, loud voice
5 the best in the world at a particular sport
6 somebody who gets paid to surf
7 at the end of a period of time
8 very big

7 SPEAKING Work in pairs. Prepare an interview with Bethany. Make notes.

Student A: You're the interviewer. Prepare five questions using the prompts below.
Student B: You're Bethany. Prepare your answers using the information in the text and your own words.

1 what / weather / like / 31 October 2003?
2 what / you / doing / when / shark / attack?
3 what / your friends / do?
4 how important / surfing / in your life / before shark attack?
5 how important / surfing / in your life / now?

8 SPEAKING Work in pairs. Act out your interview.

> What was the weather like on 31 October 2003?

Bethany Hamilton

Talking about the past

I can chat about what happened at the weekend.

1 🎧 1.19 **Complete the dialogue with phrases in the box. Listen and check.**

> my grandparents to the park some new trainers for a burger

Harry	Hi Megan. What did you do last weekend?
Megan	I went shopping on Saturday.
Harry	Really? What did you buy?
Megan	¹ _____.
Harry	Cool. What did you do on Sunday?
Megan	Nothing much. I did my homework in the morning and took the dog for a walk in the afternoon.
Harry	Where did you go?
Megan	² _____. What about you? Did you have a good weekend?
Harry	It was OK. I watched television on Saturday afternoon. Then I went out with some friends.
Megan	Where did you go?
Harry	We went ³ _____.
Megan	What did you do on Sunday?
Harry	I played computer games in the morning and visited some relatives in the afternoon.
Megan	Who did you visit?
Harry	⁴ _____.

2 SPEAKING **Work in pairs. Practise reading the dialogue in exercise 1, using different phrases from the box to complete it.**

> **1** a new top a CD some books
> **2** to the beach to the town centre round the block
> **3** to the cinema for a pizza to the park
> **4** my cousin my uncle my grandma

3 🎧 1.20 **Listen to some teenagers talking about their weekends and answer the questions.**

1 What was the score in the ice hockey match?
  a 4–3 **b** 5–4
2 What did George do on Sunday?
  a He went to the cinema. **b** He stayed in.
3 Why did Peter sit in a car for most of Saturday?
  a The beach was closed. **b** The weather was bad.
4 What did Peter do on Sunday?
  a His sister had a birthday party.
  b He did his homework and tidied his bedroom.
5 Where did Wendy go on Saturday?
  a She went to her friend's house. **b** She went shopping.
6 Why didn't she buy anything?
  a The clothes were too expensive.
  b She didn't see anything she liked.

4 **Read the speaking tip below. Underline the follow-up questions in the conversation in exercise 1.**

> **Speaking tip**
>
> When you ask someone about what they did or what happened, ask follow-up questions to find out more information and to keep the conversation going.
> **A** *What did you do on Saturday?*
> **B** *I went shopping.*
> **A** *Really? Where did you go?*

5 SPEAKING **Work in pairs. Student A: Choose an activity from the box and make a sentence using the past simple. Student B: Ask a follow-up question.**

> **Free-time activities** chat with a friend on the phone/online
> go out with my friends go to a café/to the park/to the cinema
> go away for the weekend have relatives/friends to stay
> listen to music/the radio read a book/magazine
> visit some relatives

> I went to the cinema last night.

> What did you see?

6 SPEAKING **Work in pairs. Prepare a dialogue about what you did last weekend following the chart.**

A
Greet B. Ask what he/she did last weekend.

B
Say what you did on Saturday.

Ask a follow-up question.

Answer the question.

Ask what he/she did on Sunday.

Answer the question.

Ask a follow-up question.

Answer the question.
Ask what **A** did last Sunday.

Answer the question.

Ask a follow-up question.

Answer the question.

7 SPEAKING **Act out your dialogue to the class.**

A magazine article

I can write an article for a student magazine.

1 Look at the photo. What sport is it, do you think?

2 Read the article quickly and match the headings with the paragraphs (A–D).

☐ Early successes
☐ Greatest achievements
☐ Family and early years
☐ First experience of sport

Jesse Owens

A Jesse Owens was born in 1913 in Alabama. His family was poor, and Jesse worked in his spare time to support his family.

B Jesse was a fast runner and so he joined the school athletics team. He set a new schoolboys' world record for the 100-yard sprint.

C While at university Jesse had to work to pay for his studies. He also faced racial discrimination and wasn't allowed to live with white students. On 25th May, 1935, he broke four world records within 45 minutes: the 100-yard sprint, the 220-yard sprint, the long jump and the 220-yard hurdles. He was still a student!

D At the 1936 Olympic Games Jesse won the 100-metre sprint, the 200-metre sprint, the long jump and the 400-metre relay. He also broke three Olympic records. It was a fantastic achievement.

3 Answer the questions.

1 When and where was Jesse Owens born?
2 Why did Jesse have to work in his spare time?
3 In which event did Jesse break the world record while he was still at school?
4 In what ways was university life difficult for Jesse?
5 How many world records did Jesse set on 25th May, 1935, and how long did it take him?
6 How many gold medals did Jesse win at the 1936 Olympics, and in which events?

4 Find words in the text that mean:

1 time when you are not working
2 a measure of length, used in Britain and the USA: 91 centimetres
3 a short, fast race
4 treating people badly because they are a different colour
5 a race in which the runners have to jump over small fences
6 a race between teams of runners, swimmers, etc.

Writing tip: using paragraphs

When you are preparing to write an article, divide the information into different topics. Put all the information about each topic into a separate paragraph.

5 Match the sentences about Jesse Owens with the four topics in exercise 2.

1 By the end of his first year at college, Jesse realised he could compete at the highest level.
2 Jesse was the first American to win four gold medals in a single Olympics.
3 Jesse couldn't do sports after school because he had to work.
4 When Jesse was eight, his father lost his job and the family moved to Ohio.
5 The Nazis hoped to prove at the Games that white people were physically superior to black people.
6 Jesse's school sports teacher realised that Jesse was immensely talented.
7 Jesse had nine brothers and sisters.
8 When he travelled with fellow students he had to stay in 'blacks only' hotels.

6 Write an article (130–150 words) for a student magazine about a famous sportsperson from the past (someone who has retired or died). Include paragraphs on three or four of these topics and your own ideas.

- family
- early years and education
- first experience of sport
- early successes
- greatest achievements
- why you admire him/her

Check your work

Have you
☐ divided your article into paragraphs, each with its own topic?
☐ put the paragraphs in a logical order?
☐ checked your spelling and grammar?
☐ written 130–150 words?

Language Review 1–2

Vocabulary

1 Choose the correct words.

1 I'm **optimistic / pessimistic**. I expect to have good luck.
2 He's **confident / shy**. He doesn't like talking to people that he doesn't know.
3 He's **hard-working / lazy**. He never does his homework.
4 He's **funny / serious**. He makes all his friends laugh.
5 He's **quiet / talkative**. He doesn't say much.
6 She's **kind / unkind**. She always helps people.
7 I'm **generous / mean**. I often buy presents for my friends and family.

Mark ▮ /7

2 Complete the words to make the names of sports.

1 a _ _ l _ _ _ _ _ _   4 g _ _ _ _ _ _ _ _ _ s
2 b _ _ _ a _ _   5 i _ _ _ h _ _ _ _ _ _
3 c _ c _ _ _ _ _   6 r _ _ _ _ _

Mark ▮ /6

3 Write the sports from exercise 2 in the correct group.

A play: _____, _____, _____
B do: _____, _____
C go: _____

Mark ▮ /3

Grammar

4 Choose the correct tense.

1 Dolphins **eat / are eating** fish.
2 We **often go / are often going** swimming on Sundays.
3 Look! **I wear / I'm wearing** a new jacket.
4 I can't come to your party next weekend. **I visit / I'm visiting** my grandparents.
5 Let's go out. It **doesn't rain / isn't raining** now.
6 I'm hungry. **I want / I'm wanting** a sandwich.

Mark ▮ /6

5 Complete the text with the infinitive or -*ing* form of the verbs in brackets.

Lucy Marvin lives in Hollywood. She hopes ¹_____ (be) a famous film actress one day, but at the moment she spends most of her time ²_____ (work) in a café. Last month, she agreed ³_____ (appear) in a pop video, but she usually avoids ⁴_____ (do) that kind of work because she wants ⁵_____ (be) a serious actress. She doesn't mind ⁶_____ (work) in the café, but she often imagines ⁷_____ (become) a star.

Mark ▮ /7

6 Complete the text with the past simple form of the verbs in brackets.

In 1976, Aston Villa ¹_____ (play) a football match against Leicester. Chris Nicholl, one of the Aston Villa players, ²_____ (score) four goals, but his team ³_____ (not win) because two of them ⁴_____ (be) in the wrong goal! The match ⁵_____ (finish) a 2–2 draw.

Mark ▮ /5

7 Complete the sentences with the past simple or past continuous form of the verbs in brackets.

1 I _____ (meet) a friend while I _____ (walk) to school yesterday.
2 She _____ (finish) her lunch and _____ (leave) the café.
3 He _____ (not hear) his phone because he _____ (listen) to his MP3 player.
4 I _____ (open) the curtains and _____ (look) outside; it _____ (not rain) but the sky was grey.
5 She _____ (get up) and _____ (have) a shower.
6 I _____ (not see) that goal because I _____ (not look).

Mark ▮ /6

Everyday English

8 Put the lines (a–e) in the correct order to complete the dialogue.

a Really? I can't stand computer games.
b So do I. Do you fancy watching a DVD now?
c I enjoy playing computer games.
d Sure! Good idea!
e I like watching films too.

Boy What do you like doing in your free time?
Girl ☐
Boy ☐
Girl ☐
Boy ☐
Girl ☐

Mark ▮ /5

9 Complete the dialogue with the words in the box.

about	buy	OK	see	went

Boy What did you do last Saturday?
Girl I ¹_____ to the cinema.
Boy Really? What did you ²_____?
Girl I saw the new Tom Cruise film. What ³_____ you? Did you have a good weekend?
Boy It was ⁴_____. I went shopping on Saturday.
Girl What did you ⁵_____?
Boy Some new trainers.

Mark ▮ /5

TOTAL ▮ /50

Reading

1 Look at the advert for an au pair. Find the names of:

1 the mother
2 the father
3 the son
4 the daughter

AuPairNet

We are a young family and we live in Brighton, in the south of England. We need a kind, hard-working au pair to live with us and help look after our two children, Oliver (7) and Ellie (5). Please contact us by e-mail for more information.

Jim and Sarah Wood

jimsarah@webhost.com

---

2 Read Joanna's e-mail. Match the three main paragraphs with three of the headings.

a Work experience
b Basic personal details
c Education
d Hobbies and interests
e Personality

Dear Mr and Mrs Wood,

☐ My name is Joanna Filipowska. I saw your advertisement on the AuPairNet website. I am looking for a job as an au pair in England for one year. I am 17 years old and I'm from Poznan in Poland.

☐ I think I am a kind, patient person and very hard-working. I love looking after children and I don't mind doing housework.

☐ My hobbies are films and sport. I play volleyball once a week, and I also do gymnastics at a club.

You can call me on +48 61 376 2879.

Best wishes,
Joanna

---

3 Answer the questions.

1 Where did Joanna find the advertisement?
2 Where is Joanna from?
3 How old is Joanna?
4 Which does Joanna prefer: looking after children or doing housework?
5 How often does Joanna play volleyball?
6 What other sport does Joanna do?

Writing

4 Write a short e-mail to Jim and Sarah Wood describing yourself. Include this information:

- your name and age
- where you are from
- your personality
- your hobbies and interests

Listening

5 🎧 1.21 Listen to the conversations. Number the people in the order that they first speak.

a Daniel, the neighbour
b Ellie
c Joanna
d Maria, the student
e Oliver

6 🎧 1.21 Listen again and choose the correct answer.

1 Joanna prefers **going to the cinema / watching TV**.
2 Oliver **hates / loves** playing volleyball.
3 Ellie hits the ball into the **garden next door / road**.
4 Daniel is in his **garden / house**.
5 Joanna has an English class every **day / week**.
6 Joanna thinks Daniel is good-looking **and friendly / but unfriendly**.

Speaking

7 Work in pairs. Ask and answer the questions about your partner's free-time activities.

1 How much time do you spend watching TV?
2 What about sports and exercise?
3 What else do you like doing in your free time?

> How much time do you spend watching TV?

> About an hour a day / three hours a week.

THIS UNIT INCLUDES ●●●●●
Vocabulary • rural and urban landscapes • prepositions of movement • compound nouns
• adjectives to describe places • prepositions of place • fillers • holiday activities
Grammar • *some, any, much, many, a lot of, a little* and *a few* • countable and
uncountable nouns • articles
Speaking • describing places • giving directions
Writing • a leaflet

A VOCABULARY AND LISTENING
Landscapes

I can describe a place in the town or country.

1 Look at the pictures. Where would you prefer to live? Why?

2 🎧 1.22 Label the pictures with the words in the box. Listen and check. Then check the meaning of the other words in your dictionary.

> **Rural landscapes** cottage field footpath gate
> hedge hill lane stream village wood
> **Urban landscapes** advertisement bus stop pavement
> pedestrian crossing postbox road sign roadworks
> rubbish bin street lamp traffic lights

●●●●● Vocabulary Builder (part 1): page 126

3 Label the pictures with the prepositions in the box.

> **Prepositions of movement** across over past
> through along

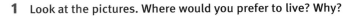

4 🎧 1.23 Listen and mark the route on the picture below.

5 SPEAKING Work in pairs. Student A: Give directions using the picture in exercise 4. Student B: Follow the directions on the picture.

> Walk along the edge of the lake … / Walk across the field to …

●●●●● Vocabulary Builder (part 2): page 126

some, any, much, many, a lot of, a few

1 Fiona is playing a computer game called *SimCity*. Read the description of her ideal town. Match the adjectives in the box with the paragraphs in the text.

> friendly   clean   exciting   attractive

Sunshine City

1 Sunshine City is a great city. There's so much to do! There are a lot of **cinemas**, **cafés**, and a few **parks** and **discos**. It's got some great clothes and music **shops** too.

2 Sunshine City is very modern and beautiful. There aren't any ugly **buildings** and there's some beautiful **scenery** around the city.

3 Is there any **pollution** in Sunshine City? There isn't much **pollution** because there isn't any **traffic**. Everyone travels by bike or walks, so there aren't many **accidents**.

4 No one works, so everyone has got a lot of free **time**. Are there any unfriendly **people** in Sunshine City? No – so come and spend a little **time** here!

2 Find two examples of *some* and four examples of *any* in the text. Then complete the rules in the *Learn this!* box.

> **LEARN THIS!**
> 1 We use _____ in affirmative sentences.
> 2 We use _____ in negative sentences and questions.

3 Martin is visiting his cousin Beth. Complete the dialogue with *some* or *any*.

Beth   Let's go to the cinema. There are ¹_____ good films on this week.

Martin   I prefer being outside. Let's go mountain-biking. Are there ²_____ hills near here?

Beth   No, there aren't.

Martin   Oh. Maybe we could go for a walk in the countryside.

Beth   There isn't ³_____ countryside near here, but there are ⁴_____ interesting parts of town.

Martin   Great. Let's go and look at ⁵_____ traffic lights.

Beth   Don't be silly. There are ⁶_____ streets in the centre where there isn't ⁷_____ traffic. You just hate cities!

4 🎧 1.24 Listen and check.

5 Look at the words in blue in the text in exercise 1. Which are plural countable nouns? Which are uncountable nouns?

6 Find *a little*, *a few*, *many*, *much* and *a lot of* in the text in exercise 1. Complete the table.

With uncountable nouns	With plural countable nouns
a lot of	3 _____
1 _____	4 _____
2 _____	5 _____

> **Look out!**
> We often use ***much*** and ***many*** in negative sentences and questions. We don't often use them in affirmative sentences. We use ***a lot of*** (or ***lots of***) in both affirmative and negative sentences.
>
> ●●●●● **Grammar Builder (3B): page 108**

7 Choose the correct words in the text.

> I live in a small village in the south of Ireland. There are ¹**much / a lot of** old houses in the village, but there aren't ²**many / much** modern buildings. There are ³**a few / a little** farms around the village. Everybody's got a car, so there is ⁴**a little / much** pollution, but much less than in the city. There isn't ⁵**many / much** entertainment, but there's ⁶**much / a lot of** beautiful scenery and it's very peaceful. I love living here.

8 🎧 1.25 Listen and check.

9 **SPEAKING** Work in pairs. Imagine you are playing *SimCity*. Describe your ideal town. Write six sentences. Use some of these words: *some, any, much, many, a lot of, a little* and *a few*.

There are a few ...
You can find some ...

10 **SPEAKING** Tell the class about your ideal town. The class votes for the best one.

CULTURE

In the country

I can understand information in a guidebook.

1 Describe the photo in the text.

2 Read the text and match the headings in the box with the paragraphs (A–D).

> industry   introduction   language   scenery

3 Read the text again. Are the sentences true or false?

1 Wales is an independent state.
2 There are 11 million people in Wales.
3 Britain's highest mountain is in Wales.
4 About 600,000 people speak Welsh.
5 More people in north Wales speak Welsh as their first language than English.
6 Sheep farmers make a lot of money.

4 🎧 1.26 Listen to a radio programme about life in north Wales. Who wants to:

1 leave north Wales?
2 stay in north Wales?
3 stay, but thinks it will be difficult?

 **a** Bryn    **b** Gareth    **c** Bethan

> *Tip*
>
> Don't take detailed notes while listening. Take short notes and use them to write full sentences later.

5 🎧 1.26 Listen again and answer the questions.

1 What is Bryn's first language?
2 What does Bryn's father do?
3 What two disadvantages of life on the farm does Bryn mention?
4 Why do tourists visit Llangollen?
5 Why doesn't Gareth enjoy living there any more?
6 What does Gareth plan to do in Cardiff or London?
7 Where is Caernarfon?
8 Why are young people leaving Caernarfon?
9 Is Bethan happy to go and live in another place?

6 **SPEAKING** Work in pairs. Ask and answer the questions.

1 What are the advantages of living in your village, town or city?
2 What are the disadvantages?
3 Have you lived in the same place all your life?
4 Do you want to live where you are now for the rest of your life? Why?/Why not?

Canol y dref
Town centre ➤

North Wales

A Wales isn't an independent state – it is part of the UK. It is situated in the west of Britain. It has a population of about three million and the capital is Cardiff. Most of the population live in the industrial south of the country.

B The north of Wales is one of the most beautiful parts of Britain. There are spectacular lakes, valleys and rivers. There are also wonderful mountains – including Snowdon, Britain's second-highest mountain.

C Two languages are spoken in Wales: English and Welsh. Welsh is a Celtic language and is one of the oldest languages in Europe. Only 20% of the total population of Wales speak Welsh, but in the small villages and towns of west and north Wales, about 75% of people speak it as their first language.

D The two main industries in the north are tourism and farming. Many people come to walk and climb in the mountains or go kayaking on the rivers. There are lots of sheep farms in the hills, but it is difficult to make money from sheep farming, and many farms are closing. Young people have difficulty finding jobs in north Wales and many of them are leaving to get jobs in the city.

Interesting fact

The village with the longest name in the world is in north Wales: Llanfairpwllgwyngyllgogerychwyrndrobwllllantysiliogogogoch. The name means: the church of St Mary in a valley of white hazel trees near a fast whirlpool by the church of St Tysilio of the red cave.

Interesting fact

There are 3 million people in Wales and 11 million sheep.

3D GRAMMAR Articles

I can correctly use 'a/an' and 'the' with nouns.

1 Look at the photo. Would you like to live in this town? Why?/Why not?

2 Read the text and match the rules in the *Learn this!* box below with the words in blue.

I live in **a** town on the east coast of England. **The** town is called Grimsby. It's **a** nice place, and I like living by **the** sea. My dad's a fisherman. He's got a big boat. I sometimes go fishing with him on the boat.

> **LEARN THIS!**
> 1 We use *a* when we talk about something for the first time. (*I've got a cat.*)
> 2 We use *the* when we talk about something again. (*I've got a cat and a dog. I like **the** dog best.*)
> 3 We use *a* when we say what someone's job is (*She's **a** doctor.*), or when we describe what somebody or something is. (*He's **a** nice man./It's **a** lovely day.*)
> 4 We use *the* when there is only one of something. (E.g. **the** sun/ **the** president)

3 Find one more example of each rule in the text.

4 Choose the best answer, *a* or *the*. Which rule applies?

MyTown.com Chatroom

Jess22	I live in ¹**a / the** small village. It's near ²**a / the** sea. It's ³**a / the** really boring place.
Dave76	Hi Jess. What's the name of ⁴**a / the** village?
Jess22	Thurlbury. It's in Scotland. Where do you live, Dave?
Dave76	Ashford.
Jess22	Is that ⁵**a / the** town or ⁶**a / the** village?
Dave76	It's ⁷**a / the** small town in ⁸**a / the** south of England. It's OK here. There's ⁹**a / the** sports centre and ¹⁰**a / the** cinema, but ¹¹**a / the** cinema's only got one screen.
Jess22	Cinema! We haven't even got ¹²**a / the** café.

> **Look out!**
> We don't use *the* when we are making generalisations.
> *What's the weather like?*
> but *I don't like hot weather.*
> *The lanes near our cottage are very narrow.*
> but *Don't drive fast in narrow lanes.*

● ● ● ● ● **Grammar Builder (3D): page 108**

5 Read the *Look out!* box. Are the sentences generalisations or not? Choose the correct answers.
1 **Life / The life** in a small village can be very boring.
2 **Weather / The weather** in Scotland was terrible last weekend.
3 This crossing isn't for **bicycles / the bicycles,** it's for **pedestrians / the pedestrians.**
4 I love **Indian food / the Indian food.**
5 **Fields / The fields** around the village are full of cows.
6 I hate **advertisements /the advertisements.** They're usually so boring.

6 🎧 1.27 **PRONUNCIATION** Listen and repeat the phrases in the box. How do we pronounce *the* before a vowel sound?

> the advertisement   the cottage   the east   the end
> the English   the gate   the industry   the scenery
> the village   the west

7 **SPEAKING** Work in pairs. Ask and answer questions using the table. Don't use *the* if it's a generalisation.

Do you like	the	big cities?
		weather today?
		scenery in your country?
		American films?
		Italian food?
		American President?
	–	original Star Wars film?
		talkative people?
		tracksuits?
		song in Unit 1?
		new iPod?
		optimistic people?

> Do you like big cities?

> Yes, I do. Do you like the weather today?

> No, I don't. Do you …

I can understand a newspaper article.

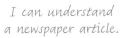

1 Look at the photos and the title of the text. What do you think it is about?

2 Read only the first sentence of each paragraph and match it with the correct topic 1–5.

1 A description of the town of Monowi
2 Finding work
3 Who is Elsie and what does she do?
4 Monowi in the past
5 What Elsie thinks of life in Monowi

3 Read the text and check your answers to exercises 1 and 2.

4 Match the highlighted adjectives in the text with the definitions below.

1 with nothing inside
2 very small
3 completely quiet
4 in the countryside
5 incredible; very surprising
6 unhappy because you have nobody to talk to
7 very big

Monowi.
Population: 1

☐ Elsie Eiler is the mayor of Monowi, a tiny town in northern Nebraska, USA. But that isn't her only job. She is also the town clerk, the town treasurer, the librarian, and she works in the bar.
5 Why has she got a lot of different jobs? Because there's nobody else to do them. Monowi has got a population of one – Elsie.

☐ Monowi is an extraordinary sight. There are about twelve old wooden houses. They are all
10 empty and are surrounded by a few trees, some old cars and lots of rubbish. The town is completely silent. An old yellow school bus, with no wheels or seats, stands next to the small school. The school closed 40 years ago. Opposite Elsie's
15 bar is an old building, filled with rubbish. It was a shop but it closed in the 1950s. Even the church has been closed since 1960.

The busiest time for Monowi was in the 1930s. Then, the population was 150, mostly farmers and
20 their families. There was a railway too. However, the farmers couldn't compete with the enormous industrialised farms. They left the town to look for other work. In 1971, the railway closed and the town began to die. Three years ago, the last inhabitant,
25 apart from Elsie and her husband, moved away. Then Elsie's husband died, and Elsie became the town's only inhabitant.

Elsie's son and daughter left years ago to find work in bigger towns. 'The small farmers and businessmen
30 can't make any money here,' says Elsie. It is the same in other small towns in the region. Between 1996 and 2004, almost 500,000 people left the rural states of Nebraska, Kansas, Oklahoma, North Dakota, South Dakota and Iowa, and went to live in big cities.

35 Now Elsie lives alone, but she isn't lonely. Her food is good, the beer is cold, and farmers and truck drivers travel a long way to eat at her café. 'One day Monowi will just be memories, and it will probably turn to dust,' she says. 'But I like it here, and as long as
40 I can take care of myself, I'll stay here.'

5 Read the text again. Are the sentences true or false? Correct the false sentences.

1 Elsie Eiler has got five jobs.
2 The shop closed first, then the church, then the school.
3 In the past it was possible to take the train to Monowi.
4 The farmers left Monowi because the railway closed.
5 Three years ago Elsie's husband moved away.
6 In this part of the USA, young people are moving from rural areas to urban areas.
7 Elsie wants to move away from Monowi.

6 Match the adjectives 1–7 with their opposites a–g.
Describing places

1	boring	a	polluted
2	clean	b	stressful
3	dangerous	c	exciting
4	modern	d	ugly
5	noisy	e	safe
6	pretty	f	old
7	relaxing	g	quiet

boring – exciting

7 Match the questions with the answers.

1 Where do you live?
2 What's it like?
3 What's the best thing about where you live?
4 What's the worst thing about where you live?
5 Would you prefer to live in the country/the city?
6 Why?/Why not?

a There are two things that I really like. It's very pretty and it's by the sea.
b I'd prefer to live in the country, but near a big town.
c I live in Kingsbridge.
d Because I like clean air and green countryside, but I also occasionally like to go shopping or see a film.
e It's a small town. There are a lot of old buildings.
f There aren't many shops and there isn't a cinema.

8 SPEAKING Work in pairs. Ask the questions in exercise 7 and give your own answers.

Giving directions

I can understand and give directions.

1 **SPEAKING** Work in pairs. Ask and answer questions about the location of shops and buildings on the map below. Use the prepositions in the box.

Prepositions of place behind   between … and   near
next to   on the corner of   opposite

Where's the sports centre?

It's opposite the clothes shop.

2 Read the dialogue and follow the directions on the map.

Woman Excuse me. Is there a bank near here?
Man Yes, there's one in Churchill Road.
Woman Can you tell me how to get there?
Man Go straight on, and, let me see, turn right at the traffic lights. Go past the cathedral and turn right into Churchill Road. The bank is opposite the bar.
Woman Thanks.

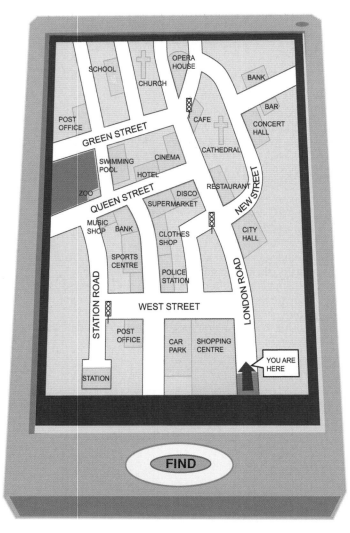

3 🎧 1.28 Listen and repeat the dialogue.

4 Match the sentences in the box with the diagrams.

Directions Go along Queen Street.   Go past the bus stop.
Go straight on.   Go to the end of the road.
Take the first left.   Turn left at the traffic lights.

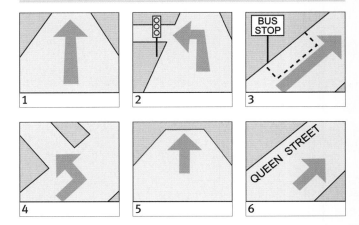

5 🎧 1.29 Listen to the dialogues and follow the directions on the map. Where do the people want to go?

6 Read the speaking tip below. Find a filler in the dialogue in exercise 2.

Speaking tip

When you need time to think during a conversation, say *let me think*, *um*, or *let me see*.

7 **SPEAKING** Work in pairs. Prepare a dialogue using the map and the chart below. Include some fillers.

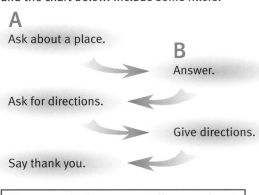

A
Ask about a place.

B
Answer.

Ask for directions.

Give directions.

Say thank you.

Excuse me. Is there a post office near here?

Yes, there's one in St. John's Street.

8 **SPEAKING** Act out your dialogue to the class.

9 **SPEAKING** Work in pairs. Ask and answer questions about how to get to places near your school.

I can write a leaflet describing places of interest.

1 Read the writing task and the two leaflets. Which place would you prefer to visit?

> **Writing task**
> Write a tourist leaflet (70–80 words) about some beautiful or interesting places in your country. Include:
> - a title to attract the readers' attention
> - information about interesting things to see and places to visit
> - information about what people can do there

A

Devon – something for everyone

Come and visit Devon, in the south-west of England. There are miles of sandy beaches, where you can swim, surf, dive or windsurf. Or just relax on the sand with a good book.

If you like walking, cycling or horse-riding, spend some time on Dartmoor, with its vast stretches of open moorland. Devon has got lots of interesting historic buildings. Visit Castle Drogo or the atmospheric castle at Totnes.

B

Visit the historic city of York

- Wander through the winding streets and walk along the ancient city walls, which are over 700 years old.

- Don't miss the famous cathedral – York Minster – which took over 300 years to build. Climb to the top of the tower and enjoy the wonderful views of the city.

- Visit the fascinating Jorvik Museum and learn about the history of York.

- Take a trip to the Yorkshire Dales and marvel at the stunning scenery.

2 Which leaflet consists of
1 a single paragraph?
2 short 'bullet points'?
Which is more effective in your opinion?

3 Divide leaflet A into three bullet points.

4 Which grammatical structure does each bullet point in leaflet B begin with?

5 Find adjectives in the leaflets that mean:
1 very big = v _____
2 important in history = h _____
3 with a special feeling = a _____
4 very old = a _____
5 well-known = f _____
6 fantastic = w _____
7 very interesting = f _____
8 very impressive = s _____

> *Writing tip*
>
> When you are writing a leaflet:
> - think of a good title to attract the readers' attention.
> - use bullet points and short, informative sentences.
> - use adjectives to make the descriptions more interesting.

6 Do the writing task in exercise 1. Include information on some of these things:
- historic towns
- beautiful landscapes
- interesting buildings
- holiday activities
- tourist attractions (e.g. museums, churches)

> *Check your work*
>
> **Have you**
> - [ ] used bullet points?
> - [ ] used short, informative sentences?
> - [ ] used a variety of adjectives?
> - [ ] written 70–80 words?

1 Get ready to SPEAK Match each word with one of the photos.

> disappointed happy lose match cyclist
> individual determination players race score
> team spirit win

2 Work in pairs. Think of some similarities and differences between the photos. Use these phases to help you.

> **Describing photos**
> Both photos show …
> In the first photo I can see … but in the second photo …

3 Do the Speaking exam task.

SPEAKING exam task

Compare and contrast the two photos. Think about these things:

1 How are the people feeling? Why?
2 How are the sports different?
3 What qualities do you need to succeed in the two sports?
4 Which of the sports would you prefer to do (if any)? Why?

4 Do the Reading exam task.

READING exam task

Read the text and match headings A–F with paragraphs 1–5. There is one extra heading that you don't need.

A The future of cheerleading   D The rules of cheerleading
B A dangerous sport   E Equipment for cheerleading
C Is it a sport?   F Two types of cheerleading

Is cheerleading a sport?
by Renee R., Arlington Heights, IL

1 Competitive cheerleading is a very popular activity for girls in the USA, but more than half of Americans do not believe it is a sport. This is because they confuse it with sideline cheerleading. These are two different activities. Sideline cheerleaders entertain the crowd during a sports match and encourage them to support their team. But in competitive cheerleading, two teams of cheerleaders compete against each other.

2 Competitive cheerleading includes lots of physical activity. Like gymnasts, cheerleaders must learn to tumble. They must be strong, and they must learn to work with other teammates. Sports like football and basketball have laws which the players follow, and so does competitive cheerleading. The cheerleaders have to stay within a certain area, and complete their routine within three minutes and 15 seconds.

3 According to the National Center for Catastrophic Sport Injury Research, cheerleading is the number-one cause of serious sports injuries to women. This is partly because they do not wear any protective gear, like helmets or knee pads. It's also because they often do not have proper training facilities – for example, they have to use a room without high ceilings or matting on the floor. Schools rarely provide good facilities because they do not recognise cheerleading as a sport.

4 So why do many people think cheerleading is not a sport? Perhaps it is because cheerleading is not a ball sport, and cheerleaders do not score points or win races. However, the same is true of wrestling, diving, gymnastics and many other sports. Perhaps it is because people see cheerleaders as entertainers, not competitors, but this is not fair; cheerleaders today compete against other teams, and they have to train hard, just like other athletes.

5 Hopefully, everybody will recognise cheerleading as a sport, just like football or basketball. It could even become an Olympic sport one day. After all, cheerleaders have to be athletic and physically fit, just like competitors in other sports.

5 Work in pairs. Answer these questions.

1 Find three reasons in paragraph 4 why some people think cheerleading isn't a sport.
2 How does the writer disagree with these people?
3 What is your opinion?

1 Get ready to LISTEN **Work in pairs. Answer the questions.**

1 Do you live in a house or a flat?
2 What rooms has it got?
3 What shops and amenities are there nearby?

2 Complete the text with the words in the box. Use your dictionary to help you.

| detached | flatmates | furnished | neighbourhood |
| neighbours | rent (v) | rent (n) | share | tube station |

I'm a student at London University. I live in a flat which I ¹_____ with two friends. It isn't our own flat; we ²_____ it. But the flat isn't ³_____ so we've got our own furniture. The flat is part of a ⁴_____ house. It's in a nice, quiet ⁵_____ and the ⁶_____ are very nice and always say hello. Luckily the ⁷_____ isn't too high, so we can afford it. My two ⁸_____ are also at London University, so every morning we walk together to the ⁹_____ and take the underground into the city.

3 🎧 1.30 **Do the Listening exam task.**

LISTENING exam task

Read sentences 1–6. You are going to hear a conversation between a student who is looking for a flat in London, and a letting agent. Choose the correct answers, A, B or C.

1 The man wants to rent a flat because he
 A is a student in London.
 B is going to stay in London for the rest of his life.
 C can't afford to buy a flat.
2 He wants to rent a flat for
 A himself only.
 B himself and two flatmates.
 C his friends.
3 He wants the flat to be
 A furnished.
 B close to the university.
 C in central London.
4 The man seems to be pleased that there is
 A a post office across the street.
 B a pub in the neighbourhood.
 C an Internet café nearby.
5 He doesn't accept the first offer because
 A the rent is too high.
 B the flat isn't furnished.
 C the neighbourhood isn't suitable.
6 He is very interested in the second offer because
 A the rent is low.
 B it's a detached house.
 C there are already four students in the house.

4 Get ready to SPEAK **Say which of these things are in the photos below.**

a notice board	e desk	i window
b poster	f shelves	j bin
c chest of drawers	g computer	k clock
d wardrobe	h carpet	l plants

5 Choose the adjectives you would use to describe the rooms.

| bright | clean | tidy | untidy | cold | cosy |
| uncomfortable | comfortable | dark | relaxing |

6 Complete the sentences contrasting the two rooms. Decide which sentence refers to which room.

| although | difference | however | the other | but |

1 The main _____ between the rooms is that one is tidy, while the other is untidy.
2 One room looks bright _____ the other is quite dark.
3 One room looks more comfortable than _____.
4 There is quite a lot of furniture in both rooms. _____, the furniture in this room is more modern.
5 _____ one room is untidier than the other, it looks cosier.

7 Do the Speaking exam task.

SPEAKING exam task

Compare and contrast the two photos. Think about these things:

1 How comfortable are the rooms?
2 Do they belong to boys or girls? Give reasons.
3 Can you tell what kind of hobbies the people have? Give reasons.
4 Which room do you prefer? Why?

4 In the spotlight

THIS UNIT INCLUDES ●●●●●

Vocabulary • types of film • adjectives to describe films • *-ed* and *-ing* adjectives
• types of TV programme
Grammar • comparatives and superlatives • *(not) as ... as*, *too*, *enough*
Speaking • talking about films and TV programmes • buying tickets
• giving opinions • checking understanding
Writing • a film review

A VOCABULARY AND LISTENING
At the cinema

I can talk about different types of film.

1 Look at the photos. Do you recognise any of the films or actors?

2 Label the photos with the words from the box. Which types of film aren't illustrated?

> **Types of film** action film   animated film   comedy
> disaster film   historical drama   horror film   musical
> romantic comedy   science fiction film   war film   western

1	
2	
3	
4	

5	
6	
7	
8	

3 🎧 1.32 Listen and check.

4 **SPEAKING** Work in pairs. What types of film do you like? What types don't you like? Give examples.

> I really like science fiction films, for example *Star Wars* and *X-Men*.

> I quite like comedies, for example ...

> I don't like ...

5 🎧 1.33 Listen to the film excerpts. What types of film are they?

6 Complete the definitions using the adjectives in the box.

> **Adjectives to describe films**   boring   entertaining   funny
> gripping   moving   scary   violent

1 You can't stop watching a <u>gripping</u> film because it's so exciting.
2 A _____ film is not at all interesting.
3 A _____ film makes you frightened.
4 A _____ film makes you laugh.
5 A _____ film makes you feel strong emotions.
6 A _____ film contains a lot of fighting and blood.
7 An _____ film is one that you enjoy watching.

7 🎧 1.34 Listen and check.

> ●●●●● Vocabulary Builder (part 1): page 127

8 Make notes about a film you really liked and a film you hated. Use adjectives from exercise 6.

> ☺ Notting Hill – funny, moving
> ☹ The Day After Tomorrow – not gripping, boring

9 **SPEAKING** Work in pairs. Tell your partner about the films. Do you agree with your partner?

> I loved *Notting Hill*. It's a romantic comedy. It was really funny and it was moving too.

> I hated *The Day After Tomorrow*. It's a disaster film. It wasn't very gripping. In fact, it was quite boring.

> ●●●●● Vocabulary Builder (part 2): page 127

GRAMMAR
Comparatives and superlatives

I can make comparisons.

1 Read the text and correct the sentences.

1 Tom Hanks is not very rich.
2 *You've Got Mail* was one of the biggest thrillers of 1998.
3 Tom Hanks is the most attractive actor in Hollywood.

Tom Hanks is one of the most famous and richest actors in Hollywood. He's won the Oscar for Best Actor twice. He can play serious roles as well as appearing in more entertaining and funnier films such as *You've Got Mail*, one of the biggest comedies of 1998. Tom Hanks isn't the most attractive actor in Hollywood, but most critics agree that he is one of the best actors!

2 Underline the comparative and superlative adjectives in the text. Complete the table.

	Comparative	Superlative
Short adjectives		
rich	richer	1 _____
big	bigger	2 _____
funny	3 _____	the funniest
Long adjectives		
entertaining	4 _____	the most entertaining
attractive	more attractive	5 _____
Irregular adjectives		
good	better	6 _____
bad	worse	the worst

3 Write sentences comparing the two films in the table. Use the comparative form of the adjectives in the box and *than*.

boring   entertaining   funny   long   popular   short   violent

The Aviator was longer than Gladiator.

	The Aviator	Gladiator
Length	170 minutes	155 minutes
Popularity	👍👍👍👍	👍👍👍👍👍
Violence	☠	☠⚔☠⚔
Entertainment	☺☺☺	☺☺☺☺
Laughs	★★★	★★

● ○ ○ ○ **Grammar Builder (4B): page 110**

4 Complete the chatroom texts with the comparative or superlative form of the adjectives in brackets.

Filmaddicts.com

Join in the chat .... *War of the Worlds*

Saw it last night. This is Spielberg's [1]_____ (good) film yet. Much [2]_____ (gripping) than his [3]_____ (early) films.
martin@hkinternet.com   posted 22.39 5 July

Are you crazy?! *Saving Private Ryan* was much [4]_____ (good)! [5]_____ (violent), yes, and [6]_____ (slow), but [7]_____ (interesting) than *WOTW*.
kate32@demonmail.co.uk   posted 22.42 5 July

I'm not a Spielberg fan. He may be Hollywood's [8]_____ (successful) director, but his films aren't [9]_____ (entertaining).
dg77@swiftmail.net   posted 22.44 5 July

How can you say that?! Name a [10]_____ (moving) film than *Schindler's List* or a [11]_____ (scary) one than *Jaws*.
kate32@demonmail.co.uk   posted 22.50 5 July

5 Complete the questions using superlative adjectives.

1 who / good-looking / actor in the world?
   Who's the best-looking actor in the world?
2 what / funny / comedy on TV?
3 who / beautiful / actress in the world?
4 what / boring / programme on TV?
5 who / good / film director in your country?
6 what / scary / film that you've ever seen?
7 what / good / film that you've ever seen?

6 **SPEAKING** Work in pairs. Ask and answer the questions in exercise 5.

In your opinion, who's the best-looking actor in the world?

Brad Pitt. Who do you think is the most beautiful actress in the world?

Scarlett Johansson. What's the funniest comedy on TV?

Look at the photos. Do you recognise the film character or the actors?

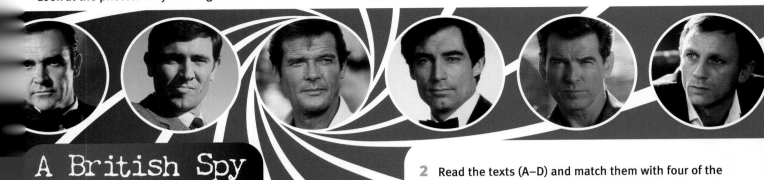

A British Spy

A ☐

The British do not make many action films. They are more famous for historical dramas and, more recently, romantic comedies like *Four Weddings and a Funeral*. However, in 1962 a film called *Dr No* appeared. It was about an intelligence agent called James Bond and was an immediate success. There are now over twenty Bond films, and they are some of the most successful action films ever made.

B ☐

Ian Fleming, the author of the James Bond books, was born in 1908, and went to Eton, one of the most expensive private schools in Britain. In the 1930s he worked as a journalist and a banker. But he wanted a more exciting life and in the Second World War he got a job in the British Intelligence Service. After the war Fleming returned to journalism, but in 1953 he started writing thrillers, using his wartime experience in the intelligence services. In all he wrote fourteen Bond books, selling millions of copies around the world. He died in 1964.

C ☐

James Bond works for MI6, the international part of the British Intelligence Service. His other name is 007 (pronounced 'double-oh seven'). In the books and early films, Bond is charming, drinks and smokes a lot, and has many affairs with women. In more recent films, he is more sensitive and less reckless, and the female characters play a bigger role in the stories. Bond is famous for the way he introduces himself: 'The name's Bond. James Bond.'

D ☐

Six actors have played the part of Bond: Sean Connery, George Lazenby, Roger Moore, Timothy Dalton, Pierce Brosnan and Daniel Craig.

2 Read the texts (A–D) and match them with four of the headings.

1 The man who created James Bond
2 British action films
3 The actors who play Bond
4 The Bond books
5 What's James Bond like?

3 SPEAKING Work in pairs. Ask and answer the questions.

1 Have you seen any Bond films? Which one(s)?
2 Did you enjoy the films? Which actors played Bond?
3 Describe James Bond's appearance and personality.
4 Name some famous film stars from your country. What types of films do they appear in?

4 🎧 1.35 Listen and complete the song from the film *The Spy Who Loved Me*. Use words from the box.

as good as	better	safe	so good	the best

Nobody does it [1]_____,
Makes me feel sad for the rest.
Nobody does it half [2]_____ you.
Baby, you're [3]_____ .

I wasn't looking, but somehow you found me.
I tried to hide from your love-light.
But like heaven above me, the spy who loved me
Is keeping all my secrets [4]_____ tonight.

And nobody does it [5]_____,
Though sometimes I wish someone could.
Nobody does it quite the way you do.
Why do you have to be [6]_____ ?

The way that you hold me, whenever you hold me,
There's some kind of magic inside you
That keeps me from running,
But just keep it coming.
How did you learn to do the things you do?

And nobody does it [7]_____,
Makes me feel sad for the rest.
Nobody does it half [8]_____ you.
Baby, baby, darling, you're [9]_____ !

1 🎧 1.36 **Read and listen to the dialogue. Answer the questions.**

1 Who is old enough to watch *Kill Bill*?
2 In Jane's opinion, which film is better, *Kill Bill* or *The Last Samurai*?
3 Why can't they see *Batman Begins*?

Jane Look. *Kill Bill* is on at the cinema.
Mike Yeah, but you have to be eighteen to see it. We aren't old enough.
Jane I'm old enough. You're not. What about *The Last Samurai*? It isn't as good as *Kill Bill*, but we can both see it.
Mike OK. I'll book the tickets online. ... Oh, no. We're too late. It's sold out.
Jane Try *Batman Begins*.
Mike That starts in fifteen minutes. There isn't enough time to get there.
Jane OK. Let's watch a DVD.
Mike All right. It's better than nothing.

2 **Complete the rules in the *Learn this!* box with *after*, *before* and *between*.**

> **LEARN THIS!**
>
> 1 An adjective comes _____ *not as* and *as*.
> (not) as good as
>
> 2 *too* comes _____ an adjective.
> too late
>
> 3 *enough* comes _____ an adjective.
> (not) old enough
>
> 4 *enough* comes _____ a noun.
> (not) enough time

3 🎧 1.37 **PRONUNCIATION** **Weak forms. Listen and repeat these sentences. How are the underlined words pronounced?**

1 It isn't <u>as</u> good <u>as</u> *Kill Bill*.
2 It's better <u>than</u> nothing.
3 There isn't enough time <u>to</u> get there.

4 **Write six sentences about yourself. Use *not as ... as* and the adjectives 1–6.**

I'm not as rich as Stephen Spielberg.

1	rich	3	short	5	talkative
2	tall	4	impatient	6	hardworking

●●●●● Grammar Builder (4D): page 110

5 **Write replies to the questions. Use *too* or *not ... enough* and the adjectives in brackets.**

1 Why don't you come to the cinema with us?
  I'm _____ . (busy)
2 Do you like the new Jim Carrey comedy?
  No. It's _____ . (funny)
3 Is it a boring film?
  Yes. It's _____ . (long)
4 Are you going to see the new Tarantino film?
  No, I can't. I'm _____ . (old)
5 Have you got *The Lord of the Rings* trilogy DVD box set?
  No, I haven't. It's _____ . (expensive)
6 Do you like war films?
  No, I don't. They're _____ . (violent)

6 **Complete the conversation between the two casting directors. Use *too*, *enough* or *as ... as* and the words in brackets.**

Martha Now, we need an actor for the lead role. Brad Peters is certainly <u>good-looking enough</u> (good-looking). But is he [1]_____ (tall)?
Max No, he isn't. He's only 1 metre 50. What about Tom Delaney? He's very attractive.
Martha But he hasn't had [2]_____ (experience). He's only acted in one film.
Max Well, Michael Lamb is [3]_____ (famous) Brad Peters – everyone knows him. He's appeared in lots of films.
Martha Yeah, but he's [4]_____ (old). He'll be 50 next year. And look at his photo – he hasn't got [5]_____ (hair). This is a romantic comedy, remember.
Max What about Dave Wilson?
Martha He's always very busy. I'm sure he hasn't got [6]_____ (time).

7 🎧 1.38 **Listen and check.**

8 **SPEAKING** **Work in pairs. Invent reasons why you can't follow the suggestions. Use *too* and *enough*.**

1 Why don't we go to the cinema?
2 Let's buy a new DVD player.
3 Shall we go to the beach?
4 Why don't we have lunch now?
5 Let's go to Paris for our holidays.
6 Why don't you study maths at university?

> Why don't we go to the cinema?

> I'm too tired. / I haven't got enough time. / The films are all too boring.

E **READING**
Crossing cultures

I can understand a profile of a famous film director.

1 Look at the photo. What do you think the man's job is?

Against the odds

Many European film directors have gone to Hollywood hoping to make their mark in the American film industry, but few have had as much success there as the
5 Czech-born film director Milos Forman.

Forman was born in 1932 in Caslav, in what is today the Czech Republic. **1** Milos never saw his parents again: they both died in concentration camps,
10 leaving him an orphan at the age of 12. Milos and his brother were brought up by one of their uncles.

After the war, Forman became fascinated by film and theatre. **2** He started out in the film industry by
15 directing television documentaries, before moving gradually into drama. He gained international recognition for *Black Peter* (1964) and was soon the leading figure in the 'golden age' of Czech cinema.

In 1967 he made his first trip to the United States, and
20 the following year went to Paris to organise the production of his first American film, *Taking Off*. **3** Not wanting to return to Czechoslovakia, Forman stayed in Paris until August 1969, when he moved to New York.

Taking Off, Forman's first English-language film,
25 appeared in 1971. The film was a critical success and won a number of awards. **4** The film became the first film for forty years to win Oscars in all five major categories – Best Film, Best Actor, Best Actress, Best Screenplay, and Best Director for Forman. In 1984,
30 Forman returned to Prague for the first time in 16 years to film scenes for *Amadeus*, which tells the life-story of the composer, Mozart. **5**

Forman's bitter experiences of totalitarian regimes, whether fascist or communist, have had a profound
35 influence on his work. **6** Naturally, Forman is always on the side of the individual.

2 Read the text quickly and answer the questions.

1 What is the man's name?
2 Where is he from?
3 Which country did he move to?
4 What are the names of three of his films?

3 Match the highlighted words in the text with the definitions below.

1 the words and directions that are written for a film
2 short part of a film, in which the action usually happens in one place
3 a prize
4 people who direct the making of films
5 a film that tells a fictional story
6 all the companies and studios that make films
7 films that give true information

Reading tip

Read the text quickly to get the general idea. Then read the missing sentences. Look for links with vocabulary before and after each gap.

4 Six sentences have been removed from the text. Choose from sentences a–g the one that best fits each gap. There is one extra sentence that you don't need.

a However, his big breakthrough came in 1975 when he directed *One Flew Over the Cuckoo's Nest*.

b He has always had to struggle to survive, and his most interesting and successful films all explore the theme of the lone individual against a hostile establishment.

c His father, who was Jewish, and his mother were arrested by the Nazis during the occupation of Czechoslovakia during the Second World War.

d The film was another huge success, winning eight Oscars, including another Best Director for Forman.

e He organised a drama club at school and went on to study screen-writing at the Film Institute at the University of Prague.

f In spite of this, he returned to Czechoslovakia the following year.

g While he was there, Russia and its Warsaw Pact allies invaded Czechoslovakia.

5 A lot of famous actors and directors move away from their home countries. Look at the photos and complete the text with the nationalities and countries in the box.

> American Austrian English Australian Welsh
> France   the USA   the UK

1 Catherine Zeta-Jones
  Nationality _____ Lives in the USA
2 Gwyneth Paltrow
  Nationality _____ Lives in _____
3 Nicole Kidman
  Nationality _____ Lives in _____
4 Alfred Hitchcock
  Nationality _____ Lived in _____
5 Arnold Schwarzenegger
  Nationality _____ Lives in _____

6 SPEAKING Work in pairs. Can you name any of the films that the people in exercise 5 acted in or directed? What types of film were they? Did you see them?

> Arnold Schwarzenegger appears in ...... films. He starred in *The Terminator*.

Buying tickets

I can buy tickets for a concert or film.

Clerk	Good evening. Can I help?
Clare	I'd like to book three tickets for *War of the Worlds*, please. The seven-thirty showing.
Clerk	Adults or children?
Clare	Two sixteen-year-olds and a thirteen-year-old.
Clerk	Sorry, did you say two thirteen-year-olds?
Clare	No, one thirteen-year-old, and two sixteen-year-olds.
Clerk	OK. That's two adults and one child. That'll be £18.
Clare	OK. Here you are.
Clerk	£20. Thank you. Here's your change.

1 🎧 **1.39 Read and listen to the dialogue above. Circle the showing that Clare books tickets for on the film guide below. Listen and repeat.**

Silver Screen Cinemas Film Guide 10–17 July

Film	Fri–Sat			Tickets
Wedding Crashers Certificate PG	18.30	20.30	22.30	Adults: £6.50
War of the Worlds Certificate 15	17.00	19.30	22.00	Children (under 14), OAPs, Students: £5
Batman Begins Certificate U	15.00	18.00		Box Office Tel: 469644
				Book online at www.ssc.co.uk

2 SPEAKING **Work in pairs. Practise reading the dialogue, changing the words in blue. Use information from the film guide.**

3 🎧 **1.40 Listen to Chris booking tickets on the phone. Answer the questions.**

1 What is Chris booking tickets for?
2 How much do they cost in total?

4 🎧 **1.40 Listen again. Mark the seats on the theatre plan and complete the credit card.**

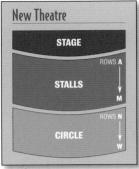

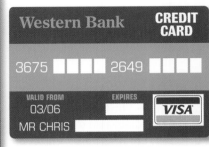

5 **Read the speaking tip below. Find one of the phrases in the dialogue in exercise 1.**

Speaking tip

Don't be afraid to say you don't understand something.
Use phrases such as:
Pardon?
Sorry, did you say …?
Could you repeat that, please?

6 SPEAKING **Work in pairs. Imagine you are booking tickets on the phone for a concert. Prepare a dialogue following the chart below.**

Clerk

Answer the phone.

Customer

Ask for tickets. Give the name of the concert, the date and number of tickets. Adults or children?

Say the prices of the seats that are available.

Say which price of seat you'd like.

Tell the customer the total price. Ask for the customer's credit card number.

Give the number.

Ask for the expiry date.

Give the expiry date.

Ask for the customer's address.

Give your address.

Thank the customer and say when you will post the tickets.

Thank the clerk and finish the call.

7 SPEAKING **Act out your dialogue to the class.**

A film review

I can write a review of a film.

1 Do you recognise the actor in the photo? Do you know the film?

2 Read the first and last paragraphs of the review. Answer the questions.

1 What is the name of the film?
2 Did the reviewer enjoy it?

A review of **War of the Worlds**   by Andrea

I recently went to see **War of the Worlds**. It's a science fiction film starring Tom Cruise.

The film is based on a book written over 100 years ago, although it is set in modern times. The story is very
5 gripping. It's about alien machines from space which land on Earth. Nevertheless, the film has a happy ending.

The acting is very good. Tom Cruise, who plays a father who is looking for his family, is excellent, as usual. However, I didn't think Dakota Fanning was very
10 convincing as his daughter. The special effects were incredible – the machines looked terrifying, and there were some very scary moments which I didn't enjoy.

This is a classic Spielberg film: fast-moving, not too violent, and full of action. In spite of the fact that it
15 was a bit scary, overall I really enjoyed it. Go and see it if you can.

3 Answer the questions.

1 What kind of film is *War of the Worlds*?
2 When was the original book written?
3 What aspects of the film did the reviewer like?
4 What two things didn't the reviewer like?

4 Find words or phrases in the review that mean:

1 with Tom Cruise as the most important actor (line 2)
2 uses the same story as (line 3)
3 acts the part of (line 7)
4 very typical; one of the best (line 13)
5 generally; when I think of everything (line 15)

5 Read the writing tip. Find and underline the words and phrases in the review.

Writing tip: expressing contrast

We use *however* and *nevertheless* to express contrast between two sentences. We put a comma after them.

We use *although* and *in spite of the fact that* to express contrast between two pieces of information in the same sentence.

6 Complete the sentences. Use words or phrases from the Writing tip above. Sometimes two answers are possible.

1 The story was good _____ I didn't like the acting.
2 I really enjoyed the film. _____ most of my friends thought it wasn't very good.
3 The special effects were very unconvincing _____ they spent millions of dollars on them.
4 I don't think Sylvester Stallone is a very good actor. _____ he's very good in the *Rocky* films.
5 The film wasn't at all funny _____ it was supposed to be a comedy.
6 The film was very slow. _____ it was quite thought-provoking.
7 *Jaws* is one of Spielberg's first films. _____ it's one of his best.
8 _____ the acting was excellent, overall I didn't enjoy it.

7 Do this writing task. Follow the writing plan below.

Write a review of a film that you enjoyed.
Write 130–150 words.

Introduction
Name of film, type of film and actors.
Paragraph 2
The story: What happens? Is it gripping? Is it convincing? What about the ending?
Paragraph 3
Other aspects of the film: the acting, the screenplay, the music, the special effects, the stunts, the location, etc.
Paragraph 4
Your overall opinion.

Check your work

Have you
☐ followed the writing plan?
☐ checked your spelling and grammar?
☐ written 130–150 words?

Vocabulary

1 Write the opposites. Choose words from the box.

attractive	boring	early	enormous	expensive
modern	polluted	rich	quiet	relaxing	safe
ugly	violent			

1 entertaining _____
2 tiny _____
3 dangerous _____
4 stressful _____
5 pretty _____
6 cheap _____
7 old-fashioned _____
8 noisy _____
9 poor _____
10 late _____

Mark ▮ /10

2 Complete the missing words.

1 A m_____ is a film with a lot of songs.
2 A c_____ is a funny film.
3 A w_____ is an area of trees.
4 A t_____ j_____ is a line of cars that can't move.
5 A p_____ c_____ is a place to cross the road safely.
6 A r_____ town is a town in the middle of the countryside.
7 T_____ l_____ tell cars when they must stop or go.
8 A r_____ b_____ is where you should put litter.
9 A h_____ d_____ is a film about people in the past.
10 A c_____ is a small, traditional house in the country.

Mark ▮ /10

Grammar

3 Rewrite the sentences using the words in brackets. Don't change the meaning.

1 My sister is more hard-working than my brother.
   (not as / lazy) My sister isn't as lazy as my brother.
2 There aren't many street lamps in the village.
   (a few) _____
3 He's too young to see that film.
   (enough) _____
4 My sister is taller than all the other people in her class.
   (tallest) _____
5 Villages are less stressful than cities.
   (relaxing) _____
6 There's a hill on one side of my house and a stream on the other.
   (between) _____
7 It's worse than his other films.
   (not as / good) _____

Mark ▮ /6

4 Choose the correct words.

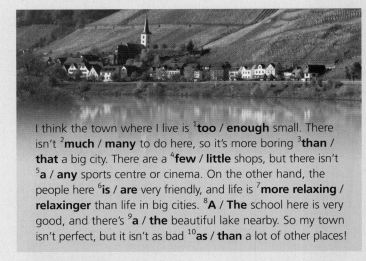

I think the town where I live is [1]**too / enough** small. There isn't [2]**much / many** to do here, so it's more boring [3]**than / that** a big city. There are a [4]**few / little** shops, but there isn't [5]**a / any** sports centre or cinema. On the other hand, the people here [6]**is / are** very friendly, and life is [7]**more relaxing / relaxinger** than life in big cities. [8]**A / The** school here is very good, and there's [9]**a / the** beautiful lake nearby. So my town isn't perfect, but it isn't as bad [10]**as / than** a lot of other places!

Mark ▮ /10

Everyday English

5 Choose the best replies (a–f) for questions 1–6.

a Yes, there is. It's on Churchill Street.
b Number 3.
c November 2010.
d Yes. Turn left at the traffic lights.
e The half past eight.
f It's behind the supermarket.

Giving directions
1 Can you tell me how to get to the city centre? ☐
2 Is there a café near here? ☐
3 Where's the car park? ☐

Buying tickets
4 Which screen is it on, please? ☐
5 Which showing would you like? ☐
6 What's the expiry date? ☐

Mark ▮ /6

6 Write the words in the correct order.

1 end / road. / Go / the / to / of / the
2 first / the / left. / Take
3 past / and / Go / hospital / the / right. / turn
4 corner / South Street. / and / It's / the / on / Park Avenue / of
5 please? / Could / repeat / you / that,
6 adult / and / One / two / children.
7 please? / have / your / card / Can / number, / I
8 you / Sorry, / say / £15? / did

Mark ▮ /8

TOTAL ▮ /50

Listening

1 🎧 **1.41** **Listen to the conversation. Why didn't Joanna see the new Tarantino film?**

  a She doesn't like action films.

  b She's too young.

  c She arrived at the cinema too late.

  d She didn't have enough money for the ticket.

2 🎧 **1.41** **Listen again. Complete the sentences with *Daniel* or *Joanna*.**

  1 _Joanna_ was going to the shop at the end of the road.

  2 _____ plays tennis.

  3 _____'s favourite films are horror films.

  4 _____ suggested going to the cinema.

  5 _____ couldn't find the cinema.

  6 _____ phoned the other person at 6.30.

  7 _____ bought a ticket and went inside.

  8 _____ arrived late at the cinema.

  9 _____ didn't buy a ticket.

Reading

3 **Read Joanna's e-mail. Number the subjects in the order she writes about them.**

  ☐ next weekend

  ☐ last weekend

  ☐ today

  ☐ Jim and Sarah's children

> Dear Chloe,
>
> Hi! How are you!
>
> I'm having a very relaxing day. I usually work on Fridays, but I'm not working today because Jim and Sarah want me to look after the children next Sunday. They're going to a rugby match in London with some friends. I don't mind working at weekends, so I agreed to do it. Oliver and Ellie are really nice children. They're very different. Oliver never stops chatting! Ellie isn't as talkative as Oliver, but I think she's more confident.
>
> I nearly went to the cinema with Daniel (the next-door neighbour) last weekend, but I was late – and then I couldn't buy a ticket because I wasn't old enough to see the film. It had an 18 certificate, you see. In the end, I had a pizza in town – on my own!! As I was leaving the restaurant, Daniel phoned me. I explained everything. He thought it was really funny!
>
> Write soon.
>
> Love
>
> Joanna

4 **Answer the questions.**

  1 Why isn't Joanna working today?

  2 What does Joanna think about working on Sundays?

  3 Who is quieter, Oliver or Ellie?

  4 In Joanna's opinion, who is shyer, Oliver or Ellie?

  5 Did Daniel phone Joanna before or after she had a pizza?

  6 How did Daniel feel about Joanna missing the film?

Speaking

5 **Work in pairs. Ask questions about your partner's weekend.**

> Did you have a good weekend?

> Yes, I did. / No, I didn't. / It was OK.

> What did you do?

> On Saturday, I …
> On Sunday, I …

Writing

6 **Write a short e-mail to a friend about the last film that you saw. Include this information:**

  • when and/or where you saw it

  • the title of the film and the name of the director and/or star

  • the type of film

  • your opinion of the film

5 Gifts

THIS UNIT INCLUDES ●●●●●
Vocabulary • shops • verbs: shopping and money • special occasions • buildings • in a shop
Grammar • present perfect • *been* and *gone* • present perfect and past simple • *How long ...?* • *for* and *since*
Speaking • giving and receiving gifts • buying clothes
Writing • an informal letter

A VOCABULARY AND LISTENING
At the shops

I can identify different shops and talk about gifts.

1 Label the photos with shops from the box. What are the people looking at or buying?

Shops	bakery	bank	butcher's	card shop

Shops bakery   bank   butcher's   card shop
chemist's   clothes shop   computer shop   electrical store
jeweller's   music shop   newsagent's   post office
shoe shop   sports shop   stationery shop   supermarket

3

1

2

4

2 🎧 1.42 Listen, repeat and check your answers in exercise 1. Check the meanings of the shops in exercise 1 in your dictionary.

3 Where can you buy these things?

a birthday cake   meat   a Christmas card   a magazine
a pair of trainers   a pair of jeans   an MP3 player   a CD
a watch   a newspaper   a ring   stamps   a tennis racquet
paper   perfume   pasta   a printer   a jacket   aspirins

4 🎧 1.43 Listen to four dialogues and answer the questions. Write your answers in the table.
1 Which shop is each person in?
   a chemist's   **b** jeweller's   **c** stationery shop   **d** bakery
2 What does each person want to buy? Choose from the things in exercise 3.
3 Does each person buy what he or she wants?

	Person 1	Person 2	Person 3	Person 4
1				
2				
3				

●●●●● Vocabulary Builder (part 1): page 128

5 **SPEAKING** Work in pairs. Talk about shops that you like going to and shops that you don't like going to. Give reasons.

> I like going to sports shops because
> I enjoy buying / looking at / trying on trainers.

> I don't like going to music shops because I'm not interested in / I hate buying / I can't afford CDs.

6 Imagine you've got 100 euros to buy gifts. Make notes.
1 Who are you going to buy gifts for? (friends / family members)
2 What gifts are you going to buy? (one or two things for each person)
3 Which shops do you need to visit?

7 **SPEAKING** Work in pairs. Tell your partner.

> I'm going to buy gifts for ... , ... and ... .
> First, I'm going to the ... to buy ... for ... .
> Then ...
> After that ...
> Finally, ...

●●●●● Vocabulary Builder (part 2): page 128

GRAMMAR

Present perfect

I can talk about recent events.

1 Read the postcard. Are the sentences true or false?

1 Amanda and Suzie have seen all the sights.
2 Amanda hasn't bought anything.
3 Suzie is with Amanda now.

Dear Dad,

We've been in New York since Sunday. We've seen all the sights and I've taken lots of photos. And of course, we've been shopping. I haven't bought very much, but Suzie has spent a fortune on presents. She's gone to Century 21, a huge clothes shop. She's been there for hours! She's just sent me a text message. She's tried on four pairs of trainers and six jackets!

Love
Amanda
P.S. Have you fed my fish?

Peter Black
3825 Lincoln Avenue
Coconut Creek
Florida 33066

2 Study the information in the box. Complete the examples from the postcard.

Present perfect
affirmative
We've _____ in New York since Sunday.
Suzie _____ spent a fortune on presents.
negative
I _____ bought very much.
interrogative
_____ you _____ my fish?

3 Underline more examples of the present perfect in the postcard. Look at the information in the *Learn this!* box. Which use do they show?

LEARN THIS!

We use the **present perfect**
1 to talk about recent events and to give news.
2 with *for* or *since* to say how long a situation has existed.

4 Study the *Look out!* box. Find an example of *been* and *gone* in the postcard.

Look out!

been and gone
We usually use *have been* instead of *have gone*. We only use *have gone* when somebody has not yet returned. Compare:
I've <u>been</u> to Paris. Do you want to see my photos?
John isn't here. He's <u>gone</u> to Paris for the weekend.

●●●●● Grammar Builder (5B): page 112

5 Complete the text messages between Suzie and Amanda. Use the present perfect form of the verbs in brackets.

Hi, Amanda. Century 21 is great! I ¹_____ (try) on four pairs of trainers and six jackets.
²_____ (you / buy) anything?

No, I ³_____. I must be careful – I ⁴_____ (spend) enough money this week! Is Mum with you?

No, she isn't. She ⁵_____ (go) to the supermarket to buy some fruit.
⁶_____ (Dad / phone) this afternoon?

I ⁷_____ (not / speak) to Dad, but I ⁸_____ (write) a postcard to him.

LEARN THIS!

1 We use *How long ...?* to ask about the length of time of a current situation.
How long have you been here?

2 We use *for* when the answer is a period of time.
I've been here for 45 minutes.

3 We use *since* when the answer is a point in time.
I've been here since 2.30.

6 Study the information in the *Learn this!* box above. Complete the sentences with *for* or *since*. Write similar sentences about yourself.

1 I've known my best friend _____ 1997.
2 I haven't had anything to eat _____ an hour.
3 I've been at this school _____ 2000.
4 I haven't bought a CD _____ last weekend.
5 I've lived in this town _____ two years.
6 I've had these shoes _____ six months.
7 We haven't had an English test _____ the end of last term.
I've known my best friend since 2001.

7 **SPEAKING** Work in pairs. Ask and answer questions with *How long ...?* and *for* or *since*. Use phrases from the box and your own ideas.

be at this school?   know me?   have that hairstyle?
live in your home?   study English?

How long have you been at this school?

Since 2002. / For five years.

I can talk about giving gifts on special occasions.

1 **Read the text. Are the sentences true or false?**

1 In the past, your 21st birthday was more important than your 18th birthday.

2 Today, people in Britain become adults at the age of 21.

3 In Britain, people have always exchanged presents on Christmas Day.

4 Parents put presents for young children in their bedrooms while they're asleep.

5 Older children open their presents with the adults.

6 People open their presents on Christmas Day in the afternoon.

7 Mothers often receive chocolates or flowers on Mother's Day.

8 When people get married, they give presents to the guests at their wedding.

2 **Look at the list of special occasions. Which do you celebrate? What other special occasions do you celebrate in your country?**

> **Special occasions** birthdays Christmas Easter Father's Day Halloween Mother's Day name days New Year's Eve Valentine's Day weddings

3 **SPEAKING** **Work in pairs.**

Student A: Interview student B about giving presents.
Student B: Interview student A about receiving presents.

Student A's questions

> Who do you buy presents for?
> On what occasions do you buy them?

> Which shops do you usually go to when you're shopping for presents?

> In your opinion, what's the best present you've ever given? Who was it for? Why was it good?

Student B's questions

> On what occasions do you receive presents? What kinds of things do you normally get?

> What's the best present you've ever received? Who gave it to you? On what occasion?

> Have you ever received a present that you really hated? What was it? Who gave it to you? What did you say?

4 **SPEAKING** **Tell the class about your partner.**

Gift-giving in Britain

IN BRITAIN, there are two occasions each year when people usually receive presents: on Christmas Day and on their birthday. In the past, your 21st birthday was the most important because it symbolised becoming an adult. People traditionally received a silver key on that day to symbolise opening the door to the adult world. Today, people in Britain legally become adults at the age of eighteen, so they often have the biggest celebration on that birthday.

The custom of giving gifts on 25 December only dates back to Victorian times. Before that it was more common in Britain to exchange presents on New Year's Eve (31 December) or Twelfth Night (5/6 January). These days, on Christmas Eve parents put presents for young children in 'stockings' and leave them in their bedrooms while they are asleep. When the children wake up in the morning, many of them believe that Santa Claus has visited them in the night and brought them their presents. Gifts for older children and grown-ups are put around the Christmas tree on Christmas Eve. Then, on Christmas morning, everyone sits around the tree and opens their presents.

Easter and Mother's Day are also important days. Young children usually receive chocolate eggs at Easter, and people often give presents (usually chocolates or flowers) to their mothers on Mother's Day. People also receive gifts on important occasions in their lives. For example, all the guests at a wedding traditionally bring a gift for the bride and groom. And these days, students sometimes get presents from their parents if they do well in their exams!

Present perfect and past simple

I can talk about past experiences and when they happened.

1 🎧 1.44 **Read and listen to the dialogue. Are the sentences true or false?**

1 Both Sue and Mark have listened to Green Day.
2 Both Sue and Mark like Green Day's music.
3 Both Sue and Mark have seen Green Day in concert.

Mark	Have you ever **listened** to Green Day?
Sue	Yes, **I have**. I **got** their latest album last weekend for my birthday. It's great.
Mark	**I've seen** them in concert.
Sue	Really? **Were** they good?
Mark	Yes, fantastic. They **played** all my favourite songs.
Sue	Lucky you! **I've never been** to a rock concert.

2 Which tense are the verbs in blue, present perfect or past simple?

3 Study the information in the *Learn this!* box. Why are the verbs in the dialogue past simple or present perfect?

> **LEARN THIS!**
>
> 1 We use the **present perfect** to talk about an experience at any time in the past. The exact time of the experience isn't important.
> *I've seen the latest James Bond film.*
> *Have you ever been to France?*
>
> 2 We use the **past simple** to talk about a specific occasion in the past.
> *I saw the latest James Bond film last night.*
> *Did you go to France last summer?*

●●●● **Grammar Builder (5D): page 112**

4 Choose the correct tense.

1 I usually get great Christmas presents from my family, but **I've received / I received** a few bad ones too!
2 It was my birthday last week, and my parents **have given / gave** me a digital camera.
3 We went out for dinner last weekend. **We've had / We had** pasta.
4 I love Chinese food, but **I've never eaten / I never ate** Japanese food.
5 She's a Russell Crowe fan. **She's seen / She saw** all his films.
6 We went to the cinema last night. **We've seen / We saw** a Tarantino film.

> **Look out!**
>
> *present perfect* and *past simple*
> We often use the **present perfect** to ask and answer questions about an experience, and then the **past simple** to give more information about a specific occasion.
> *'Have you ever been to Japan?'*
> *'Yes, I have. I went there last summer.'*

5 Study the information in the *Look out!* box. Then complete each dialogue with one verb from the box. Use the present perfect and the past simple.

eat	find	~~forget~~	meet	see

1 A <u>Have you ever forgotten</u> somebody's birthday?
  B Yes, I have. I <u>forgot</u> my brother's birthday last year.
2 A _____ a Woody Allen film?
  B Yes, I have. I _____ *Scoop* a few weeks ago.
3 A _____ a famous person?
  B Yes, I have. I _____ David Beckham when he visited our school.
4 A _____ Indian food?
  B Yes, I have. In fact, I _____ chicken curry last night.
5 A _____ money on the pavement?
  B Yes, I have. I once _____ £10.

6 🎧 1.45 **Listen and check.**

7 Complete the questions with the past participle of the verbs in brackets.

Have you ever ...

1 _____ (buy) anything in a department store?
2 _____ (have) an argument with your parents?
3 _____ (borrow) money from someone?
4 _____ (hear) a really funny joke?
5 _____ (receive) a present you didn't like?
6 _____ (see) a rock concert on TV?
7 _____ (forget) to do your homework?

8 **SPEAKING** **Work in pairs. Ask and answer the questions. If the answer is yes, give more information using the past simple.**

Have you ever bought anything in a deparment store?

Yes, I have. I bought a jacket in C&A last month.

1 Look at the reading tip below. Read the texts and find out which of the three buildings is:

1 the oldest
2 the newest
3 the highest

> ### Reading tip
>
> To locate specific information in a text, look out for key words which will help you find the information you need. For example, information on height or age is likely to contain numbers, dates and words such as *metres*, *metres high*, *years* and *years old*.

2 Look at the reading tip below. Match the highlighted words in the texts with the definitions below.

a a building of any kind
b the shape of tall buildings against the sky
c home (formal word)
d land around a large building
e an open part of a building, high up
f the act of building something
g a tall thin building or part of a building
h a large room for dances and parties
i a very large room for formal meetings
j a special occasion when people walk through the streets

> ### Reading tip
>
> If there is a word in the text you don't understand, try to guess its meaning from the context.

Taking liberties

Since 1886, the Statue of Liberty has been one of the most famous monuments in America – in fact, the world. The statue was a gift to the USA from the French people. They built the statue in France, then carried it across the Atlantic Ocean in 350 pieces and re-built it in New York. They completed the work in 1886, and about a million people watched the opening parade on 28 October of that year. At the time, the Statue of Liberty was the tallest structure in New York, at 93 metres. Since then, they have built many taller buildings, but the Statue of Liberty is still an impressive sight, and millions of visitors have climbed the 354 steps to the top.

From Russia with love

Poles either love it or hate it. The Palace of Culture and Science has dominated the Warsaw skyline for over 50 years, and is still one of the tallest buildings in Europe. It was a personal gift from Joseph Stalin to the Polish people. 3,500 building workers from the former Soviet Union came to Warsaw, and construction lasted from May 1952 until July 1955. It stands 231 metres high and has got 3,288 rooms including three theatres, a swimming pool, a museum and a congress hall for 3,000 people. It is now one of the most popular tourist attractions in Warsaw and every year thousands of people visit the terrace on the 35th floor and enjoy the views across the city.

3 Choose the best answers.

1 They built the Statue of Liberty
  a in New York.
  b in France from pieces made in New York.
  c in France and then carried it across the Atlantic in many pieces.
  d in Russia.

2 The construction of the Palace of Culture and Science took
  a over 50 years.
  b 231 days.
  c over three years.
  d 35 years.

3 People visit the Palace of Culture and Science
  a to go swimming.
  b to visit the museum.
  c to look at the views of the city.
  d for a variety of work and leisure reasons.

4 The castle we can see today at Balmoral
  a is the original castle.
  b is a new castle, built in 1856.
  c is the original castle, but with a new tower.
  d is too small for the royal family.

5 Today, Balmoral Castle is
  a a tourist attraction and the Queen's home in Scotland.
  b just a tourist attraction.
  c a private home for the Queen and her family.
  d a place for visitors to have dances and parties.

4 SPEAKING Work in pairs. Think of three other famous buildings in the world. Answer the questions.

1 What kind of building is it? Choose from the words in the box.
2 Where is it?
3 In which century did they build it?

Buildings castle cathedral City Hall concert hall government building museum opera house palace skyscraper stadium temple tower

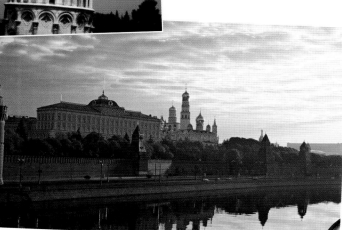

Queen of the castle

Balmoral Castle was a present for Queen Victoria from her husband, Prince Albert, in 1852. The countryside around the castle is spectacular, and includes Lochnagar, a mountain 1,160 metres high. The royal couple decided that the original castle was too small, so they built a new one. They completed it in 1856, with a beautiful tower about 30 metres high. The castle and its grounds have belonged to the British royal family since that time, and each new generation has improved the property. Today, the Queen and her family always stay at Balmoral when they visit Scotland. The castle has been open to the public for over 35 years, but visitors can only enter the ballroom – the other rooms are the Queen's private residence.

EVERYDAY ENGLISH
Buying clothes

I can go shopping for clothes.

1 Complete the dialogue with words from the box.

£24.99	black	brother	jumper	jumpers	medium

Shop assistant Can I help you?
Julia Yes, I'm looking for a ¹_____ .
Shop assistant The ²_____ are over there, near the changing rooms.
Julia OK. Thanks ... This one's nice. And it's in the sale! Have you got it in ³_____ ?
Shop assistant Yes. What size are you?
Julia It isn't for me. It's a present for my ⁴_____ . He's a ⁵_____ , I think.
Shop assistant Here you are. Could you come over to the till, please? That's ⁶_____ .
Julia Can I bring it back if it doesn't fit?
Shop assistant Sure. Just keep the receipt.

2 🎧 1.46 Listen and repeat, copying the intonation.

3 Find the words in the dialogue and match them with the definitions.

In a shop	changing room	receipt	sale	size
till	to fit			

a a time when a shop sells things for less money than usual
b how big or small something is
c the place in a shop where you pay for things
d a place where you try on clothes
e the ticket you get when you buy something
f to be the right size

Exam tip

Go to the *Functions Bank* in the Workbook for more phrases and expressions you can use in a conversation.

Talking about prices
We write	We say
75p	*Seventy-five p*
£15	*Fifteen pounds*
£4.99	*Four pounds ninety-nine* or *four ninety-nine*

4 **PRONUNCIATION** Study the information in the box above, then say the prices.

1 £2.50	4 £45
2 50p	5 £10.99
3 £19.95	6 95p

5 **SPEAKING** Work in pairs. Practise reading the dialogue in exercise 1, using different words from the box to complete it.

(1,2) T-shirt(s)   jacket(s)   tracksuit(s)
(3) blue   green   yellow
(4) sister   boyfriend/girlfriend   cousin
(5) small   large   extra-large
(6) £15.95   £35   £19.50

6 🎧 1.47 Listen to two dialogues and complete the table.

	Article of clothing	Size	Colour
Dialogue 1			
Dialogue 2			

Exam tip

Look at the table before you listen to the recording. Make sure you know what information you are listening for.

7 Complete the sentences from the dialogues.
1 _____ are you?
   Um, small, I think.
2 Can I _____ ?
   Of course. The changing rooms are over there.
3 Can I help you?
   Yes, I'm looking for a top _____ this skirt.
4 How much are they?
   The _____ is on the label.
5 _____ it in a 14?
   I'll just have a look.

8 🎧 1.48 Listen and check.

9 **SPEAKING** Work in pairs. Imagine you are in a clothes shop. Prepare a dialogue using the ideas below. Make notes.
- What is the customer looking for?
- Colour?
- Size?
- Try it on? Does it fit?
- Price?

10 Write your dialogue out. Practise reading it in pairs.

11 **SPEAKING** Act out your dialogue to the class.

An informal letter

I can write an informal thank-you letter.

1 Read the letter. Find three things that Amy got for her birthday.

2 Find colloquial words and phrases in the letter that mean:

1 beautiful
2 to look good with something
3 to return something
4 the USA
5 I think ...
6 aeroplane
7 friends
8 very good

3 Put what Amy says in the correct paragraph and in the correct order.

a She says that she enjoyed her birthday.
b She says what Sophie gave her.
c She thanks her aunt for the scarf.
d She says what her parents gave her.
e She thanks her aunt again for the scarf.
f She says why she likes the scarf.
g She says how often she's worn the scarf.

Paragraph 1	Paragraph 2	Paragraph 3
1 _____	4 _____	7 _____
2 _____	5 _____	
3 _____	6 _____	

4 Read the writing tip below. What expression does Amy use to end her letter?

Writing tip

When you write an informal letter:
- put your address in the top right-hand corner
- put the date below your address
- start the letter *Dear ...*
- you can use colloquial language
- finish the letter with *Love* or *Best wishes* and your name.

5 Imagine that you have received a present from a friend or family member. Choose a present from the box (or use your own idea) and say why you like it.

an MP3 player   a CD   a book   a DVD   some money
some make-up   a necklace or earrings   a bag
some pens   a mobile phone

6 Write an informal thank-you letter of 120–150 words. Use the plan to help you.

Paragraph 1
- Say thank you. Say what the present is and say something about it: What's it like? Why do you like it? Have you used it?

Paragraph 2
- Say what you did on the special occasion. Say what other presents you received.

Paragraph 3
- Say thank you again.

14 Northbrook Road
Oxford OX1 4RH

24th March 2007

Dear Aunt Susan,

Thank you so much for the scarf that you sent me for my birthday. It's gorgeous! It's very warm and the colour really goes with my eyes. I've worn it every day for the last week. Sophie wanted to borrow it yesterday, but I didn't lend it to her – she never gives things back!

I really enjoyed my birthday. Mum and Dad gave me some money because I'm saving for a holiday in the States. (I reckon I've nearly saved enough for the plane ticket!) Sophie gave me a DVD of *The Two Towers*, the second film in *The Lord of the Rings* trilogy. Have you seen it? I haven't watched it yet, but my mates say it's brilliant.

I hope you're well. Thanks again for the lovely scarf!

Lots of love

Amy

Check your work

Have you
- ☐ laid out the letter correctly?
- ☐ used informal language?
- ☐ included all the information in the task in exercise 6?
- ☐ written 120–150 words?

1 Match three of the events with the reviews.

disco   play   film   football match   ice show
rock concert

2 Do the Reading exam task.

READING exam task

Choose the best answers, A, B, C or D.

1 Before the show Sally had to wait because
   A there were a lot of other people waiting to get in.
   B she went to the wrong building.
   C she was twenty minutes late.
   D she couldn't find her seat.
2 The best thing about the show was
   A the costumes.
   B the first-class skaters.
   C the lighting.
   D the finale.
3 Jake went to see *Romeo and Juliet* because
   A the tickets were very cheap.
   B his friends were going.
   C his teacher said it would be a good idea.
   D he loves the play.
4 Jake enjoyed
   A reading the play in class.
   B the acting, but not the language.
   C reading it more than seeing it on stage.
   D seeing it on stage more than reading it.
5 Katie was disappointed because
   A *MetalHead*'s performance only lasted an hour.
   B the support band were better than *MetalHead*.
   C she didn't recognise any of the songs they played.
   D her boyfriend wasn't impressed.
6 Who does Katie think will enjoy the concert?
   A Everyone.
   B Only people who really like *MetalHead*.
   C People who can afford expensive tickets.
   D People who like loud music.

Ⓐ The Ice Show at the Nottingham Ice Centre features some of the world's top skaters and they certainly put on a first-class display.
I arrived early and had to join a long queue right round the building, so it was twenty minutes before I got to my seat. I bought a programme, which was packed with information about the skaters. However, it was rather expensive at £10.
Apart from those small complaints, everything else was fantastic. The standard of skating was excellent, as you'd expect, and the costumes and lighting were wonderful.
What I enjoyed most was the finale, when all the performers danced together and received a standing ovation from the audience. If you want to see this show, book your tickets quickly before they sell out.

Sally, 15

Ⓑ We are studying **Romeo and Juliet** at school and our English teacher suggested we go and see a production of it at the Queen's Theatre. The tickets were very cheap, so I went with some of my friends. Shakespeare's language is sometimes quite difficult to understand so I didn't enjoy reading the play in class very much. However, seeing it performed on stage was a completely different experience. It was much easier to understand. I thought the acting was really good, too. I'd recommend this play to anybody!

Jake, 17

Ⓒ Last night I went with my boyfriend to see **MetalHead** at the Arena. They are his favourite band but I wasn't that impressed. I thought the support band **Flight** were excellent – but **MetalHead** didn't appear till well after ten o'clock, and then only played for an hour. The band played all their best-known hits, though, and had the audience jumping to their feet and dancing. Personally, I thought it was too loud. Fans of **MetalHead** probably won't be disappointed (though the tickets were very expensive), but if you're not keen on heavy metal music played at high volume, this is not the concert for you.

Katie, 16

3 What would and wouldn't you enjoy about these events?

4 Get ready to SPEAK **Put phrases 1–8 into the correct groups.**

1 I'd love to.
2 Why don't we ...?
3 I'm not keen on (+ noun or -*ing* form)
4 Let's ...
5 That's a good idea.
6 I'd rather ...
7 I don't really want to ...
8 I'd prefer to ...

Making suggestions
1 _____   2 _____
Expressing dislikes
1 _____   2 _____
Expressing preferences
1 _____   2 _____
Accepting suggestions
1 _____   2 _____

5 Do the Speaking exam task. Use the phrases in exercise 4 to help you.

SPEAKING exam task

You and your friends want to go to one of the events in exercise 1. Agree on an event. Think about:

1 what you would enjoy about each event
2 what you wouldn't enjoy about each event
3 the cost

1 Complete the sentences with the words in the box.

> ages   clothes   money   shopping   shops

1 How often do you go _____?
2 Do you like going round the _____ with your friends?
3 Do you enjoy trying on _____?
4 Do you spend a lot of _____ on CDs?
5 Do you get annoyed if people spend _____ deciding what to buy?

2 Get ready to LISTEN Work in pairs. Ask and answer the questions in exercise 1.

3 🎧 1.49 Do the Listening exam task.

LISTENING exam task

Read sentences A–F. Then listen and match them with the speakers (1–5). There is one extra sentence that you don't need.

A I don't like looking at things in shop windows.
B I never go shopping with my boyfriend.
C I like shopping more than my boyfriend does.
D I mostly buy the things I need online.
E I never go shopping alone.
F I don't go shopping very often but when I do, I spend a long time in certain shops.

Speaker 1	
Speaker 2	
Speaker 3	
Speaker 4	
Speaker 5	

4 Get ready to SPEAK Complete the sentences with the words in the box.

> cash   cheaper   choice   faulty   leave   touch
> shop assistant   time

1 You can see and _____ the goods.
2 You don't have to _____ the house.
3 There is usually a wider _____ of goods.
4 You can easily return _____ goods.
5 You can pay in _____.
6 Goods are usually _____.
7 You can shop at any _____ you like.
8 You can ask a _____ to help you.

5 In your opinion, which sentences in exercise 4 refer to shopping online and which to real shops?

6 For each sentence in exercise 4 make two sentences using these phrases.

> One advantage of ... is that ...
> One disadvantage of ... is that ...

One advantage of real shops is that you can see and touch the goods. One disadvantage of online shopping is that you can't see and touch the goods.

7 Answer the questions about each photo.
1 Where are the people?
2 What are they doing?

8 Do the Speaking exam task.

SPEAKING exam task

Compare and contrast the two photos. Which is better, shopping in shops or shopping online? Give reasons. Think about:

1 convenience
2 cost
3 seeing the things you want to buy
4 delivery
5 returning faulty goods

6 Technology

THIS UNIT INCLUDES ●●●●●
Vocabulary • electronic devices • phrasal verbs • mobiles: verb + noun phrases • places
Grammar • *will* and *going to* • zero conditional • *may, might* and *could*
Speaking • making predictions • arranging to meet
Writing • a formal letter

A VOCABULARY AND LISTENING
Useful gadgets

I can describe electronic devices.

1 Look at the photos. Which of the devices have you used in the last week?

1 _____

4 _____

3 _____

5 _____

6 _____

2 Label the photos with words from the box. Which devices aren't illustrated?

> **Electronic devices** calculator camcorder digital camera digital radio DVD player games console hard disk recorder mobile phone MP3 player portable CD player satellite TV stereo video recorder

3 🎧 2.01 Listen, repeat and check your answers. Check the meanings in your dictionary.

> ●●●●● Vocabulary Builder (part 1): page 129

4 Which devices belong to one or more of the groups (a–c)? Which don't belong to any?

a You can listen to music on it.
b You can record or watch moving pictures on it.
c You can play games on it.

5 🎧 2.02 Listen to four radio advertisements. Which devices from exercise 2 are they advertising?

> ### Exam tip
>
> Listen for key words to help you understand the discussion. Try to predict some of the words you might hear before you listen.

6 SPEAKING Work in pairs. Which three devices from exercise 2 do you think are the most useful? Why?

7 SPEAKING Tell the class what you think. Vote for the three most useful devices.

> ●●●●● Vocabulary Builder (part 2): page 129

7 _____

8 _____

will and *going to*

I can make predictions, offers, promises and decisions.

1 🎧 2.03 Listen to the dialogue and choose *will* or *going to*.

Debra Where's the map?
Rick I didn't bring it. ¹**I'm going to** / **I'll** use my new mobile phone instead. It's got a satellite navigation system.
Debra OK, fine. So where are we?
Rick Just a minute. I'm trying to switch it on.
Debra Well, hurry up. I'm getting cold.
Rick ²**I'm going to** / **I'll** lend you my coat.
Debra Thanks. We're lost, aren't we? And look at that black cloud. ³**It's going to** / **It'll** rain. What are you doing?
Rick I'm hitting my phone. It isn't working.
Debra Do you think ⁴**that's going to** / **that'll** help?
Rick Probably not.
Debra Look, I've got a better idea. ⁵**I'm going to** / **I'll** call a taxi.
Rick But we don't know where we are!

2 Study the information in the *Learn this!* box. Match examples 1–5 of *will* and *going to* in the dialogue with the uses in the box.

We use **will** for
1 Predictions, especially after *I (don't) think ...*
I think he'll like his present.

2 Offers and promises
I'll lend you some money.
I won't tell anyone.

3 Decisions that you make while you are speaking
He isn't answering his phone. I'll send a text.

We use **going to** for
4 Predictions, especially when they're based on what we can see
Look out! You're going to drop that computer!

5 Intentions
I'm going to work hard next term.

●●●●● Grammar Builder (6B): page 114

3 Complete the speech bubbles with the correct form of *will* or *going to*.

Oh no! We ¹_____ hit that tree!

What tree?

Oh no! I've dropped my money!

Don't worry! I ²_____ pick it up for you!

Oh no! My camera!

Don't worry. I ³_____ buy you a new one, I promise.

Why are you wearing those clothes?

I ⁴_____ tidy my room.

It ⁵_____ be another bad day for business.

4 🎧 2.04 PRONUNCIATION Listen and repeat the answers to exercise 3. How is the word *to* pronounced in *going to*?

5 Make notes about your own future. Write down:
- three things you're going to do next week
- three things you think you'll do after you leave school

6 SPEAKING Work in pairs. Tell your partner your intentions and predictions from exercise 5. Are any the same as your partner's?

1 Look at the photos in the text and the title. What does 'txt' mean? Why is it written like this?

2 Read the text. Which paragraph (1–3) mentions:

1 a TV show?
2 a school essay?
3 an addiction?
4 the fastest texter in the world?
5 e-mails?
6 a mobile phone company?
7 the language of text?
8 competitions?

3 Work in pairs. Try to say these words and phrases from text messages. How would you write them in normal English?

1 cu soon
2 call me b4 2moro
3 ur gr8
4 i luv u
5 im @ home

4 🎧 2.05 Listen to four teenagers talking about how they use a mobile phone. Answer the questions.

| Paula | Ethan | Darren | Cindy |

1 Who loves texting?
2 Who loves ringtones?
3 Who has got a 3G phone?
4 Who talks for a long time on the phone?

5 🎧 2.05 Listen again. Complete the phrases with the nouns in the box. Translate them.

> handset   number   ringtone   text message   voice call
> wireless headset

Mobiles: verb + noun phrases

1 upgrade a _____
2 make a _____
3 use a _____
4 dial a _____
5 download a _____
6 send a _____

6 SPEAKING Work in pairs. Ask and answer the questions.

1 How often do you use a mobile phone?
2 What do you use it for?
3 What do you think you will use it for in the future?

The joy of txt

1

The British love sending text messages. They send more than 2.5 billion every month. And most people now understand the language of text, with its numbers and missing letters. In fact, when a student at a Scottish school wrote an essay entirely 'in txt', his teacher gave him 'C+ 4 f4t' ('C+ for effort').

2

Although texting is a convenient and cheap method of staying in touch with your friends, it can also bring problems. In 2005, a British teenager became the first person in the world to receive treatment for an addiction to text messaging. In one year, the nineteen-year-old spent about £4,500 on texts. (He was sending about 700 texts a week.) He was also addicted to e-mail, and sent 8,000 messages in one month from his computer at work. The treatment is working well, however, and he now spends no more than £10 a week on texts.

3

For some people, text messaging has changed their lives. For example, James Trusler from Sussex in England travels around the world taking part in texting competitions and TV shows. He's the world's fastest texter and recently set a new world record while he was appearing on Australian TV. He texted: 'The razor-toothed piranhas of the genera Serrasalmus and Pygocentrus are the most ferocious freshwater fish in the world. In reality they seldom attack a human.' It took him 67 seconds. (That's fast. Try it!) James sends a lot of text messages – about 2,500 a month. Fortunately, he doesn't get big bills because he works for a large mobile phone company!

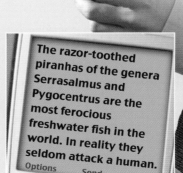

The razor-toothed piranhas of the genera Serrasalmus and Pygocentrus are the most ferocious freshwater fish in the world. In reality they seldom attack a human.
Options   Send   Clear

6D GRAMMAR
Zero conditional

I can talk about outcomes and possibilities.

1 Read the text about the Truth Machine. Which lights come on if a person tells a lie?

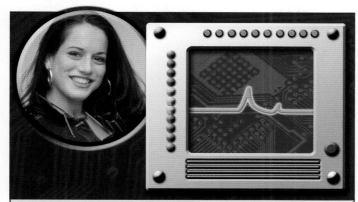

If you tell a lie, your voice contains signs of stress. You can't help it! This gadget is called the Truth Machine. It measures the amount of stress in a person's voice. **If the person is very relaxed, the green lights come on.** The red lights come on if there is some stress in the voice.

2 Look at the sentences in blue in the text. Which tense do we use in the *if* clause? Which tense do we use in the main clause? Complete the rules in the *Learn this!* box.

> **LEARN THIS!**
>
> **1** We use the **zero conditional** to talk about a result which always follows from a particular action. We use the _____ to describe the action and the _____ to describe the result.
>
> **2** The *if* clause can come before or after the main clause. If it comes after, we don't use a comma.
> *Your voice contains signs of stress if you tell a lie.*

⦿●●●● Grammar Builder (6D): page 114

3 Work in pairs. Can you complete the facts? Use the zero conditional.

1 If you heat water to 100° Celsius, …
2 If you dial *#06# on your mobile phone, …
3 If you mix blue paint and yellow paint, …
4 If you mix green light and red light, …
5 If you leave a fish out of water, …
6 If you multiply 1111111 by 1111111, …

4 Complete the sentences with information that is true for you. Use the zero conditional.

1 My teacher gets annoyed if …
2 I don't sleep very well if …
3 I speak more in English classes if …
4 I go to bed late if …
5 I feel happy if …
6 I get angry if …

5 SPEAKING Work in pairs. Compare your sentences from exercise 4. Are any of them the same?

may, might and *could*

6 Read the text and underline all the examples of *may, might* and *could*. Which two are negative?

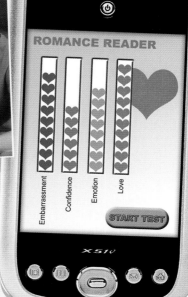

Imagine a boy is talking to a girl he secretly loves. But how does she feel about him?

She may love him too, or she may not even like him. How can he find out? Ask her? That could be embarrassing for both of them and she might not give a true answer. No, this boy needs the Romance Reader. Load the software onto a pocket PC, press 'start' and just chat to the person you are interested in. The Romance Reader listens and tells you how he or she really feels about you. It might be the start of a big romance …

7 Study the information in the *Learn this!* box. Complete the rules.

> **LEARN THIS!**
>
> **1** To talk about possibility in the present or future, we can use *may, might* or *could* followed by the infinitive without *to*.
> *They may/might/could be at home now.* (present)
> *She may/might/could buy a new DVD recorder.* (future)
>
> **2** We use *may not* or _____ *not* for the negative. We don't use _____ *not*.

8 SPEAKING Tell your partner something that you:

• might do this evening
• may not remember to do next week
• could have in your pocket or bag
• may eat this evening
• might not enjoy doing tomorrow
• could wear tomorrow

⦿●●●● Grammar Builder (6D): page 114

Nanotechnology

I can understand an article in detail.

1 Do you agree or disagree with this statement? Give reasons.

Technology is making the world a better place.

2 Read the text. Which paragraphs contain the information to complete the sentences? Complete them in your own words.

  1 Nanobots could make the world a much better place because scientists might be able to ...

  2 Nanobots could make the world a much worse place because they might ...

3 Match the highlighted words in the text with the definitions below.

  1 very small
  2 a bad dream
  3 an imaginary situation
  4 a vehicle that can travel underwater
  5 the world around us
  6 a person who goes to see a doctor
  7 whole, complete
  8 to make a person who is ill better
  9 very frightening

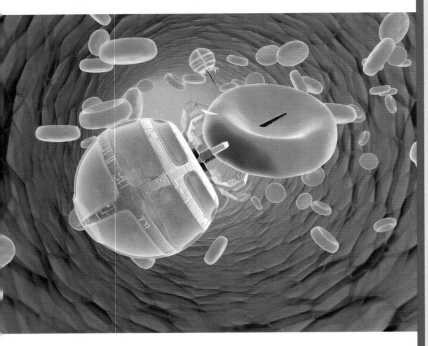

Exam tip

In true/false tasks, read each sentence then look for the information in the text. Underline the words in the text that give you the answer and compare them with the sentences in the exercise.

What's the big idea?

When people try to make predictions about the future, they usually get them completely wrong, like the prediction made by T.J. Watson, the head of IBM, in 1943: 'I think there may be a market
5 for five computers in total in the world.' Today, about 45 million PCs are sold every year in the USA alone.

Nanotechnology is the science of building tiny machines, so small that you cannot see them. Most scientists agree that nanotechnology will change our lives in the future –
10 but how? It's difficult to predict whether this new technology will be like a wonderful dream, or a terrifying nightmare.

The dream

In the 1966 science fiction film *Fantastic Voyage*, an inventor develops an amazing new way to cure diseases. He makes a group of scientists and their submarine
15 incredibly small and injects them all into a patient. They then travel around the body of the patient, visiting the different parts and repairing them. Of course, this is just a fantasy – but the reality of nanotechnology is not very different. Scientists are already making nanobots, tiny
20 robots that are smaller than a virus. In the future, doctors might be able to inject these into a patient, and the nanobots will travel around the body and repair any damage. They'll be able to cure almost every disease.

The nightmare

Some people are worried that nanotechnology could be
25 difficult to control. Nanobots might escape into the environment and damage people, plants and animals. Others have even more serious worries. Eric Drexler is a futurist, a scientist who makes predictions about the future. In his book, *Engines of Creation*, he predicted the
30 invention of nanobots. He also described a special kind of nanobot that can make a copy of itself using the materials around it – and this is where the nightmare begins. In Michael Crichton's book *Prey*, nanobots make copies of themselves so quickly that they use all the
35 materials around and then look for more ... and more, and more, eventually 'eating' the world. Some people are worried that this might really happen. The most extreme predictions (which very few scientists believe) say that nanobots could destroy the entire planet in about
40 three hours!

4 Read the text carefully. Are the sentences true or false?

1 T.J. Watson was correct about the future of the PC.
2 Most scientists think that nanotechnology will be important in the future.
3 It's easy to predict how nanotechnology will affect our lives.
4 In 1966, an inventor developed an amazing new way to cure diseases.
5 In the future, scientists might be able to cure diseases by injecting nanobots into patients.
6 Eric Drexler invented nanobots.
7 Most scientists are worried that nanobots could destroy the world in about three hours.

5 SPEAKING Work in pairs. Look at the photos and decide which of the inventions have:

1 made the world better.
2 made the world worse.
3 made no difference.

Give reasons for your answers.

> **Tip**
>
> To express your opinion, use phrases and expressions such as:
> *I think (cars have made the world better/worse) because …*
> *In my opinion, … because …*
> *On the other hand, …*

a satellite

a robot

a computer

a CCTV camera

a digital watch

a nuclear weapon

a car

Arranging to meet

I can make arrangements to meet somebody.

1 🎧 2.06 **Read and listen to the dialogue. When and where are Justin and Tracey going to meet?**

Justin   Hello?
Tracey   Hi, Justin. It's Tracey.
Justin   Hi, Tracey. What are you up to?
Tracey   Nothing much. Do you fancy meeting up in town?
Justin   Sure. What time?
Tracey   About four o'clock.
Justin   OK. Where do you want to meet?
Tracey   Why don't we meet at the department store?
Justin   Fine. I'll see you at four.
Justin   Just a moment. Where are we going to meet, exactly?
Tracey   Let's meet outside the main doors.
Justin   OK, great. See you later!

2 SPEAKING **Work in pairs. Practise reading the dialogue using your own names and changing the words in blue. Use words and phrases from the box and your own ideas.**

> **Place**   leisure centre   bookshop   sports centre
>
> **Exact meeting point**   by the lifts / escalators / stairs
> just inside the main doors / side entrance
> in the coffee bar

3 Find three different ways of making a suggestion in the dialogue in exercise 1.
1 _____ meeting up in town?
2 _____ meet at the department store?
3 _____ meet outside the main doors.

4 🎧 2.07 **Listen to the dialogue. Why don't Tracey and Justin meet at four o'clock?**

Exam tip

Don't worry if you can't understand every word in the recording. Just keep listening.

5 🎧 2.07 **Listen again. What is their new arrangement? Circle the correct information in the table.**

Time	Place	Exact meeting point
4.15	the sports shop	by customer services
4.30	the library	by the back door
5.00	the music shop	on the top floor
5.30	the museum	on the ground floor

6 SPEAKING **Work in pairs. Prepare a dialogue following the chart below.**

A
Greet B.
Suggest meeting up in town.

B
Agree. Ask what time.

Reply.

Agree. Suggest a place to meet.

Agree. Ask for a meeting point.

Confirm time, place and meeting point.

Agree. End conversation.

7 SPEAKING **Act out your dialogue to the class.**

6G WRITING
A formal letter

I can write a letter of complaint.

1 **SPEAKING** Work in pairs. Student A: Read the first letter. Student B: Read the second letter. Ask and answer the questions.

1 What is the name of the gadget?
2 Where did she buy it?
3 When did she buy it?
4 What is the problem with it?
5 What does she want the company to do?

---

11 Wood Close
Newcastle NE13 7TY

14th May 2007

Customer Services Department
Zenon Electronics
London SW12 7OP

Dear Sir or Madam,

I am writing to report a fault with the new Zenon ZK400 MP3 player that I bought from The Gadget Shop in Newcastle on 28th April.

It sometimes stops in the middle of a track. To make it start, I have to turn the MP3 player off and then turn it on again.

I am returning the MP3 player to you with this letter. I would be grateful if you could repair the fault. If this is not possible, could you please send me a new MP3 player?

I look forward to hearing from you.

Yours faithfully
Madeline Connor
Madeline Connor

---

23 Marston Rd
Bolton BO12 4FG

3rd January 2008

Customer Services Department
Computers Online
Manchester M5 5HJ

Dear Sir or Madam,

I am writing to complain about an UltraFast modem that I recently bought from your website.

When it arrived, I connected it to my PC, but it does not work. I cannot access the Internet or send e-mails.

I am enclosing the modem together with the receipt. Could you please replace the modem as soon as possible?

I look forward to hearing from you.

Yours faithfully
Victoria Swift
Victoria Swift

---

2 Read the letters. In which paragraph does each writer:

1 explain the problem in detail?
2 say why she is writing the letter?
3 say what she wants the company to do?

3 Complete the rules for formal letters with the words in the box.

> *Dear Sir or Madam*   date   full name   *Yours faithfully*

1 Write the ¹_____ in full, e.g. *14th May 2007*.
2 Start the letter *Dear Mr/Mrs/Miss*, etc. if you know the name of the person you are writing to, or ²_____ if you don't.
3 Do not use colloquial language or slang, e.g. *My **mum** bought me a CD player, and it's **rubbish**.*
4 Finish the letter with *Yours sincerely* if you used the person's name at the start, or ³_____ if you didn't.
5 If you type the letter, include your ⁴_____ at the end of the letter after your signature.

4 Read the writing tip below. Underline the set phrases in the letters.

> ### Writing tip
>
> We often use these set phrases in formal letters:
> *I am writing to …*
> *I would be grateful if you could …*
> *Could you please …?*
> *I look forward to hearing from you.*
> *I am enclosing …*

5 Imagine that you have bought one of the electronic devices on page 54. Then choose a fault from the ideas in the box below or invent your own.

> you can't turn it off   the pictures are black and white
> there's no sound   it's very slow   you can't switch it on
> you can't play your old CDs / DVDs / games on it

6 Write a formal letter of 130–150 words to the manufacturer using your ideas from exercise 5. Include this information:

- Say what the gadget is called, and where and when you bought it.
- Say what the problem is.
- Tell the company you are returning the gadget. Ask them to repair it or send you a new one.

> ### Check your work
>
> **Have you**
> ☐ followed the rules for formal letters in exercise 3?
> ☐ included all the information in the task in exercise 6?
> ☐ checked your spelling, punctuation and grammar?
> ☐ written 130–150 words?

Vocabulary

1 Complete the shops (1–7) and match them with the things that you can buy there (a–g).

1 b__k__ry ☐
2 b__tch__r's ☐
3 ch__m__st's ☐
4 j__w__ll__r's ☐
5 n__ws__g__nt's ☐
6 p__st __ff__ce ☐
7 __l__ctr__c__l st__r__ ☐

a sausages
b a watch
c a magazine
d camcorder
e bread
f stamps
g aspirins

Mark ▮ /7

2 Complete the gadgets with the words in the box.

camera	console	phone	player	recorder	TV

1 digital _____
2 MP3 _____
3 games _____
4 mobile _____
5 satellite _____
6 hard disk _____

Mark ▮ /6

Grammar

3 Complete the dialogue with the present perfect form of the verbs in the box.

be	buy	do	enjoy	have	not rain	spend	visit

It's the last day of Peter's holiday in London.
Cath [1]_____ you _____ your holiday in London?
Peter Yes, I have. I [2]_____ a great time.
Cath What [3]_____ you _____?
Peter I [4]_____ lots of interesting places, like the Tower of London and Madame Tussauds.
Cath [5]_____ weather _____ good?
Peter Yes, it has. It [6]_____ at all!
Cath [7]_____ you _____ any souvenirs?
Peter No, I haven't.
Cath Why don't you go shopping this afternoon?
Peter Because I [8]_____ all my money!

Mark ▮ /8

4 Complete the e-mail with the present perfect or past simple form of the verbs in brackets.

Dear John
How are you? Thanks for the New Year's Eve party – I [1]_____ (have) a great time. I [2]_____ (meet) some nice people too. Your friend Mike was really friendly. I [3]_____ (give) him my phone number, but he [4]_____ (not call) me yet. [5]_____ you _____ (speak) to him since your party? (Don't tell him I asked!!)
[6]_____ you _____ (see) the new Brad Pitt film? I [7]_____ (see) it last night. It's brilliant!
Tamara

Mark ▮ /7

5 Complete the mini-dialogues with the correct form of *will* or *going to*.

1 A The red top is £8, the blue top is £9.
 B I _____ have the red top, please.
2 A Have you got any plans for the weekend?
 B Yes. I _____ visit my friends in Brighton.
3 A It's really hot in this room.
 B OK. I _____ open the window.
4 A Is the match nearly over?
 B Yes, this might be the last point. Roger Federer _____ win.
5 A See you later.
 B OK. I _____ give you a call tomorrow.
6 A Are you on holiday next week?
 B Yes. I _____ stay in bed all morning on Monday!

Mark ▮ /6

6 Complete the sentences with the words in the box.

don't	if	have	might	might not	comes on

1 She gets angry _____ you interrupt her.
2 I may phone you if I _____ time.
3 If Liverpool don't score quickly, they _____ win.
4 If I press this button, a light _____.
5 I could fail my exam if I _____ work hard.
6 If she isn't at home, she _____ be in town.

Mark ▮ /6

Everyday English

7 Number the lines of the dialogue in the correct order.

☐ Yes. I'm looking for a jacket.
☐ This one's nice. Have you got it in green?
☐ Can I help you?
☐ No, we haven't. Sorry.
☐ The jackets are over there, near the window.

Mark ▮ /5

8 Write the missing words to complete the dialogue.

Boy Hi! What are you [1]_____ to?
Girl Nothing much. Do you want to meet up [2]_____ town?
Boy Sure. Why [3]_____ we meet at the café?
Girl [4]_____ time?
Boy About one o'clock.
Girl OK. [5]_____ meet outside the main doors.
Boy Good idea.

Mark ▮ /5

TOTAL ▮ /50

Reading

1 Read the information about Brighton. Match the paragraphs with three of the headings.

A Shopping
B Places to stay
C Entertainment
D History
E Transport

1 Brighton began as a small village. In 1500, there were only five streets: North Street, South Street, East Street, West Street and Middle Street. There were a few cottages by the sea for fishermen , but there weren't any large buildings. Around 1750, people from London started to visit towns on the south coast because they believed that the sea was good for their health. Brighton became very popular. By 1875, it was a large town with a museum, a library, a hospital and a royal palace . Today, it is a city with a population of nearly 250,000.

2 Brighton is a great place for music fans. Some of the most fashionable clubs in the UK are in two streets in Brighton, West Street and Kings Road Arches, and well-known DJs often perform there. Every year in May, the Brighton Festival offers a programme of theatre, dance, classical concerts and opera. If you prefer other forms of entertainment, there are many museums, art galleries and theatres in Brighton. You can also see films at the oldest independent cinema in the UK, The Duke Of York.

3 If you're interested in fashion, Brighton is the ideal place to shop. There are some large department stores, and also lots of smaller, independent clothes shops. These often sell more unusual clothes. The most famous area for shopping in Brighton is The Lanes. Here you can buy interesting jewellery, hats, shoes, perfume and all sorts of other things. There are also open-air markets where you can find great bargains !

2 Answer the questions.

1 How big was Brighton in 1500?
2 Why did people start to visit the town around 1750?
3 Where can you find the most fashionable clubs?
4 What kind of music can you hear at the Brighton Festival?
5 What's the most famous shopping area in Brighton called?
6 Which sells more unusual clothes: the department stores or the independent shops?

3 Match the highlighted words in the text with the definitions below.

1 famous
2 not part of a big company
3 men who go fishing as a job
4 outdoors
5 things that you can buy for a good price
6 a building for a king or queen, or their family
7 perfect

Listening

4 🎧 2.08 Listen to the conversations. Joanna is shopping in Brighton. What does she buy Oliver for his birthday?

a a T-shirt
b a robot dog
c a pen / radio

5 🎧 2.08 Listen again and choose the correct answer from the numbers in the box.

| 3 | 8 | 9 | 11 | 95 | 350 |

1 How old is Oliver going to be next week?
_____ years old.
2 What time do Maria and Joanna arrange to meet?
_____ o'clock.
3 How much is the T-shirt that Joanna looks at?
£_____ .
4 How many words does Robo Dog know?
_____ words.
5 How much is Robo Dog?
£_____ .
6 How much is the pen?
£_____ .

Writing

6 Imagine that a relative has given you one of the presents in the box as a birthday present. Write a short thank-you note. Include the following information:

• what the present is
• when you have used it / worn it
• why you like it

| a T-shirt | a pen | RoboDog | an MP3 player |
| a digital camera | a sweatshirt | | |

Speaking

7 Answer the questions. Make notes.

1 Do you prefer giving presents or receiving them? Why?
2 What kind of presents do you usually receive?
3 Do you think money is a good present? Give reasons.

8 Work in pairs. Ask and answer the questions in exercise 7.

7 Cultures and customs

THIS UNIT INCLUDES ●●●●●
Vocabulary • gestures • phrasal verbs • social activities
Grammar • *must, mustn't* and *needn't* • first conditional
Speaking • making, accepting and declining invitations
Writing • a note

A VOCABULARY AND LISTENING
Body language

I can describe how people greet each other in different countries.

1 Look at the pictures. Describe how the people are greeting each other. Use expressions from the box.

> **Gestures** beckon bow cross your legs fold your arms
> hold hands hug kiss nod pat somebody on the back/head
> point (at somebody/something) shake hands
> shake your head wave wink

2 🎧 2.09 Listen and repeat all the gestures, doing them as you say them. Mime the ones that involve another person.

3 Which of the gestures and greetings in exercise 1 do people use in your country?

> They often shake hands.

> They rarely …

●○○○ Vocabulary Builder (part 1): page 130

4 🎧 2.10 Listen to three people talking about customs in their country. Match the two halves of the sentences.
1 Lucy thinks that Australian people are …
2 Haruko thinks that Japanese people are …
3 Ludmila thinks that Russian people are …

a quite formal and very polite.
b very warm and friendly.
c informal and treat everyone the same.

5 Choose the correct words.
1 In Australia, you **should** / **shouldn't** sit in the front of a taxi.
2 In Australia, it's rude to wink at a **man** / **woman**.
3 In Japan, you shouldn't **cross your legs** / **fold your arms** when you're in a formal situation.
4 In Japan, you **should** / **shouldn't** kiss a woman on the cheek when you meet her for the first time.
5 When you visit a Japanese house, you shouldn't look in the **kitchen** / **bathroom**.
6 In Russia, men **and** / **but not** women greet each other in public with a hug.
7 In Russia, close friends kiss **twice** / **three times** when they meet.

6 🎧 2.10 Listen again and check.

7 SPEAKING Work in pairs. Answer the questions.
• Do you kiss/hug people you see every day?
• Do you kiss/hug friends and family that you haven't seen for a few weeks?
• Do you shake hands with people when you meet them for the first time?
• Do you use any other forms of greeting (for example, a 'high five')?

●○○○ Vocabulary Builder (part 2): page 130

GRAMMAR
must, mustn't and needn't

I can talk about prohibition and necessity.

1 🎧 **2.11** Listen and complete the text with *must*, *mustn't* or *needn't*.

How to be polite at a Chinese meal

You ¹_____ start your food until the host picks up his or her chopsticks. In general, if your host offers you food, you ²_____ accept it. (It's better to leave it in your bowl than refuse it.) Periods of silence during a meal are not considered embarrassing in China, so you ³_____ talk just to fill the gaps. As the Chinese proverb says: 'Your speech should be better than silence. If not, be silent.'

2 Study your answers to exercise 1. Complete the rules in the *Learn this!* box with *must*, *mustn't* or *needn't*.

> **LEARN THIS!**
> 1 We use _____ to express **necessity** (something that is very important to do).
> 2 We use _____ to express **lack of necessity** (something that isn't necessary but isn't against the rules).
> 3 We use _____ to express **prohibition** (something that is very important not to do).

●●●● Grammar Builder (7B): page 116

3 Write sentences about your school with *must*, *mustn't* and *needn't*. Use phrases from the box.

> run in the corridor   study English   copy your friend's homework switch off your mobile phone in class   wear a uniform stand up when the teacher comes in

At our school we mustn't ...

4 Work in pairs. How many more sentences can you make about rules in your school?

5 Complete the facts about customs around the world with *must*, *mustn't* or *needn't*.

1 In many Arab countries, you _____ arrive on time for meetings or social events – punctuality is not considered important.
2 In many parts of Asia, you _____ touch or pat somebody on the head – it is considered offensive.
3 In many Asian countries, you _____ eat with your right hand because your left hand is considered dirty.
4 In many countries, you _____ use your index finger to beckon somebody – it is very rude.
5 If you are invited to somebody's home in Brazil, you _____ take a gift, but it's normal to send a thank-you note the next day.
6 In most Asian countries, you _____ remove your shoes before entering somebody's house – it is offensive to wear them indoors.
7 In Indonesia, you _____ use a knife and fork at mealtimes – you can use your fingers if you prefer.
8 In most European countries, you _____ belch at the table because it's rude. However, in Arab countries it is a compliment.

6 **SPEAKING** Work in pairs. Think about the customs in your country when you visit somebody's house for a meal. Are the ideas in the box things you *must* do, *mustn't* do or *needn't* do?

> arrive exactly on time   belch at the table   bring flowers take your shoes off when you enter the house eat everything that you are given   eat with your fingers eat with a knife and fork

7 Write a short note to somebody who is visiting your country. Explain how to be polite when you go to somebody's house for a meal. Use your ideas from exercise 6.

Hi _____,
Here's some advice about how to be polite when you go to somebody's house for a meal.
You must ...
You mustn't ...
You needn't ...
Best wishes

_____

Thanksgiving in the USA

Americans celebrate Thanksgiving every year on the fourth Thursday in November. It's a very important festival for families, who usually come together for a long weekend – even if some of them have to travel long distances to get home. According to American tradition, the first Thanksgiving took place in 1621, soon after the first European settlers arrived in North America.

The most common meal at Thanksgiving in the USA is roast turkey and vegetables. According to tradition, the person who gets the 'wishbone' must break it and make a wish. Of course, you needn't have turkey at Thanksgiving. Lobster and crab are also popular.

Apart from the family meal, the Thanksgiving weekend is also a time for sport, parades and shopping. There are American football matches on TV, as well as college football matches around the country. In New York, the department store Macy's organises a famous fancy-dress parade which always ends with Santa Claus. The Friday of Thanksgiving weekend is traditionally a busy shopping day because people start to buy presents for Christmas.

Traditionally, autumn festivals are an occasion to give thanks for having plenty of food. However, Thanksgiving is also an opportunity to remember those people who are less fortunate. In many US cities, volunteers spend some of the holiday working in soup kitchens which distribute free food to the poor and homeless.

1 Read the text. Which of the activities is *not* mentioned?

- dancing
- eating a big meal
- shopping
- spending time with your family
- volunteering for charity work
- watching a parade
- watching sport

2 Read the text again and answer the questions.

1 When was the first Thanksgiving, according to American tradition?
2 What is the most common meal at Thanksgiving?
3 Who has to make a wish at the meal?
4 Where is Macy's parade?
5 Why are the shops busy on the Friday after Thanksgiving?
6 How do volunteers help less fortunate people?

3 🎧 2.12 Listen to the story of the first Thanksgiving dinner. Why did the Pilgrims want to thank the Native Americans?

Exam tip

Read the task carefully before you listen to the recording. This way you will find out what the recording is about and it will be easier to understand.

4 Put the events of the story in the correct order.

a ☐ The Pilgrims had a good harvest.
b ☐ Many of the Pilgrims became very ill.
c ☐ Ninety Native Americans had dinner with the Pilgrims.
d ☐ The Pilgrims went to North America.
e ☐ Squanto and Samoset gave the Pilgrims advice.
f ☐ The Pilgrims met two Native Americans: Squanto and Samoset.
g ☐ The Pilgrims invited the Native Americans to a special meal.

5 🎧 2.12 Listen again and check.

6 **SPEAKING** Work in pairs. Choose a festival that you both like. Ask and answer the questions about how it is celebrated. Tell the class.

1 What do young children usually do?
2 What do teenagers and adults usually do?
3 Is there any special food?
4 Why do you like this festival?

1 SPEAKING Work in pairs. Answer the questions.

1 Do you know any superstitions?
2 Do you believe in any superstitions?
3 Do you know anyone who is very superstitious? How does it affect their behaviour?

2 Read the text. Are any of the superstitions familiar to you?

Superstitions

Some superstitions are part of British culture. If a black cat walks in front of you, you will have good luck. On the other hand, you will have seven years of bad luck if you break a mirror. A lot of people don't really believe in superstitions, but at the same time, nobody likes to take chances: if you look at the seats on some aeroplanes, you won't find the number 13. According to a survey, people who believe in superstitions have worse luck than people who don't believe in them. In other words, if you believe in bad luck, you'll probably have it!

3 Study the information in the *Learn this!* box. Look at the *if* clauses and main clauses in blue in the text above and underline two more examples.

> **LEARN THIS!**
>
> 1 We use the **first conditional** to predict the result of an action. We use the present simple to describe the action and *will* + verb to describe the result.
>
> *If a black cat walks in front of you, you will have good luck.*
>
> ⬆ action ⬆ result
>
> 2 The *if* clause can come before or after the main clause. If it comes after, we don't use a comma.
>
> *You will have bad luck if you break a mirror.*

●●●● Grammar Builder (7D): page 116

4 Complete the sentences about superstitions around the world. Use the present simple or *will* form of the verbs in brackets.

1 (UK) If a cat washes behind its ears, it _____ (rain).
2 (Venezuela) If you _____ (give) somebody handkerchiefs as a gift, you won't have a good relationship with that person.
3 (Brazil) If you eat lentils on 1st January, you _____ (make) a lot of money during the year.
4 (Korea) If a man _____ (smile) a lot during his wedding, his first child won't be a boy, it will be a girl.
5 (Turkey) If you see a spider in your house, you _____ (have) visitors.
6 (Thailand) If a woman _____ (sing) in the kitchen, she will marry a very old man.

5 🎧 2.13 PRONUNCIATION Listen and repeat the sentences in exercise 4. How are the words *will* and *won't* pronounced?

6 Complete the text with the correct form of the verbs in brackets.

Superstitions around the world

a magpie

Different countries have different superstitions. For example, in England, it's unlucky to see one magpie on its own, but in Korea, it's the opposite. If you ¹_____ (see) a magpie in the morning, you ²_____ (get) good news that day. Another Korean superstition says that you mustn't wash your hair on the morning of an exam. If you ³_____ (wash) it, you ⁴_____ (not remember) what you've learned!

In Russia, mirrors can be lucky or unlucky. If you ⁵_____ (look) in a broken mirror, you ⁶_____ (have) bad luck. If you ⁷_____ (leave) something at home by mistake and have to go back for it, you ⁸_____ (have) bad luck. But you ⁹_____ (not be) unlucky if you ¹⁰_____ (look) in a mirror when you go home to get it.

a broken mirror

Sometimes, cities have their own superstitions. At Salamanca University in Spain, there is a superstition about a stone carving on one of the walls. If students ¹¹_____ (touch) this carving before a test, they ¹²_____ (do) well. But if they ¹³_____ (forget) to touch it, they ¹⁴_____ (not pass) the test.

the stone carving at Salamanca University

7 SPEAKING Work in pairs. Ask and answer the questions.
What will you do if:
• you can't sleep tonight?
• it rains all weekend?
• you can't do your homework?
• you feel ill tomorrow?
• there's nothing good on TV this evening?

> What will you do if you can't sleep tonight?

> I'll read a book.

1 Look at the photos. What are the people doing? Why do you think they are doing it? Use the title and headings of the texts to help you.

The traditions they tried to ban

Water throwing festival

The weather in Thailand is very hot in spring, but if you are visiting that country in April, it might be a good idea to take an umbrella and a raincoat with you. Every year on 13 April, which is New Year in Thailand, there is a water throwing festival. Young people run or drive through the streets with buckets of water or enormous water-guns and throw water at anybody they see. So, if you don't want to get wet, don't stand in the street. Participants must follow three important rules. Firstly, they mustn't throw water at old people. Secondly, they mustn't touch people. Thirdly, they mustn't throw water at car drivers. Every year people get killed or injured in road accidents during the festival. Some people are concerned about the number of casualties and want to ban the festival. However, the festival is a big tourist attraction, and will probably continue for many years.

Cheese rolling

Nobody knows exactly when this tradition at Cooper's Hill in the centre of England started, but it was hundreds of years ago. The rules are simple: you have to chase a large, round cheese down a very steep hill. This dangerous event takes place every year at the end of May. Participants often break arms or legs, and even the spectators are at risk : one year, a cheese jumped into the air and hit a 59-year-old grandmother on the head. 1997 was a particularly bad year for casualties . Up to 37 people were hurt, so in 1998, the local authorities banned the cheese rolling. However, because of all the protests, the ban only lasted a year and the tradition started again in 1999. To reduce the number of injuries, participants and spectators had to follow a few simple safety rules. Now, only about twelve people a year get injured!

2 Match the sentences to the three festivals. Write WT for Water Throwing, CR for Cheese Rolling or BR for Bull Running.

1 Nobody knows when the tradition began.
2 Old people don't take part.
3 It was banned because too many people got injured.
4 It's part of a longer festival.
5 It takes place at eight o'clock in the morning.
6 It takes place on the same day every year.
7 Participants have to chase something.
8 Participants have to throw something.
9 Participants have to escape from something.

3 Match the highlighted words in the text with the definitions below.

1 in danger
2 large containers for carrying water
3 make smaller
4 people who take part in something
5 worried
6 write your name on a list
7 people who get hurt
8 hard, pointed things on an animal's head
9 people who watch something

4 SPEAKING Work in pairs. Each choose one of the festivals in this lesson. Read the questions below, then spend a few minutes reading about the festival again. Close your books and tell your partner about the festival. Your partner checks the answers are correct.

1 Where and when does it take place?
2 What happens?
3 What do you think of the festival?

Bull running

It is the most famous part of the Fiesta de San Fermín, a week-long festival that is held every July in Pamplona, Spain. Every morning at eight o'clock, participants run through the streets in front of a group of six bulls, each about 600 kg. Anybody can take part. You needn't sign up – you just have to stand in the street and wait for the bulls. But it's a dangerous event. In 2004, eight participants were injured when the bulls caught them with their horns.

All spectators must stay behind the double line of fences along the road. This is because the participants need to jump over the first line of fences into an empty space to escape from the bulls. Each year, there are people who want to ban the bull running. They aren't concerned about the number of injuries to the participants – they're protesting because, after the bull running, the bulls are killed in bull fights.

Olivia	I'm having some friends over tomorrow night to watch a DVD. Would you like to come?
Katie	I'd love to, thanks. What time?
Olivia	About eight o'clock.
Katie	Shall I eat before I come?
Olivia	No, we're going to eat while we watch the film.
Katie	Shall I bring some food, then?
Olivia	You needn't bring anything. I'm going to make some popcorn too!
Katie	Great! I love popcorn.
Olivia	See you tomorrow.
Katie	Bye!

1 🎧 **2.14 Read and listen to the dialogue. Are the sentences true or false?**

1 Katie accepts an invitation to Olivia's house.
2 Olivia asks Katie to bring some popcorn.
3 Katie doesn't like popcorn.

2 🎧 **2.15 Listen and complete the invitations in the table with activities from the box.**

Social activities go for a bike ride   go shopping
go skateboarding   go to the cinema   have a barbecue
have a party   have lunch in a café   meet friends
play basketball   play computer games
~~watch a football match~~   go to a rock concert

Invitation to ...	
1	watch a football match
2	
3	
4	
5	
6	

3 🎧 **2.15 Listen again. Do the speakers say yes or no?**

1 – yes

4 🎧 **2.16 Listen and repeat the phrases in the box. Try to copy the intonation.**

LEARN THIS!

Invitations

1 *Making*
Would you like to come?
Do you fancy joining us?
Why don't you come along?

2 *Accepting*
I'd love to, thanks.
Yes. That sounds great!
Thanks. I'll definitely be there.

Reacting
Great! See you there.
Glad you can make it.

3 *Declining*
I'm sorry, I can't.
I'd love to, but I can't.
Sorry, but I won't be able to make it.

Reacting
That's a shame.
Sorry you can't make it.

5 **SPEAKING** **Work in pairs. Prepare two short dialogues, following the chart below. Use ideas and phrases from the *Learn this!* box and exercise 2.**

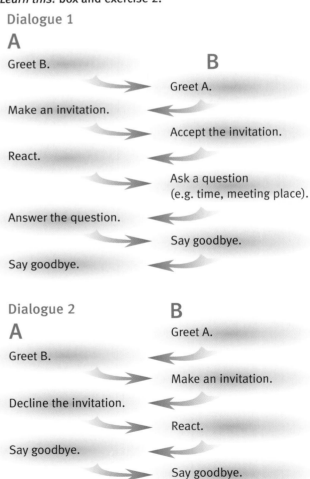

Dialogue 1

A
Greet B.

Make an invitation.

React.

Answer the question.

Say goodbye.

B
Greet A.

Accept the invitation.

Ask a question (e.g. time, meeting place).

Say goodbye.

Dialogue 2

A
Greet B.

Decline the invitation.

Say goodbye.

B
Greet A.

Make an invitation.

React.

Say goodbye.

6 **SPEAKING** **Act out your dialogues to the class.**

WRITING

A note

I can write a note replying to an invitation.

1 Read the notes. Which note is (a) making, (b) accepting and (c) declining an invitation?

① Hi Janet,
Thanks very much for your note. It's very kind of you to invite me to your Halloween party, but I'm afraid I won't be able to **make it**. My grandparents are coming to visit us that weekend. It's my grandma's birthday on Saturday, and we're going for dinner at Giovanni's in Church Rd. It's **too bad**, because I love Halloween parties!
Anyway, I hope you have a great party!
See you soon
Louise

② Dear Jack,
It's my birthday next Sunday and I'm going to have some **mates** round. Would you like to come? If the weather's good, we'll have a barbecue in the back garden. There'll be lots of burgers, chicken, crisps, etc. so you needn't bring any food. Just bring a few CDs. I haven't got many, and my sister's CDs are **rubbish**!

Hope you can make it.

Mike

PS RSVP asap! Tel. 643492

③ Hi Tania,
Great to **hear from you**. And thanks very much for the invitation to your fancy dress party on New Year's Eve. I'll definitely be there!
I'm already thinking about my costume.
'Hollywood' is a great theme. I'm really looking forward to it!
Love
Gloria

PS Shall I bring some food, e.g. crisps?

2 Answer the questions.
1 What kind of party is Janet having?
2 What is Louise going to do on the evening of Janet's party?
3 What is Louise's opinion of Halloween parties?
4 How is Mike going to celebrate his birthday?
5 What does Mike want Jack to bring?
6 What day of the year is Tania's party?
7 What is the theme of Tania's party?

3 Match the words in the box with the abbreviations.

and so on	as soon as possible	compact disc	for example
I also want to say	Please reply	Road	telephone number

1 CD	3 Tel.	5 RSVP	7 PS
2 Rd	4 e.g.	6 etc.	8 asap

Exam tip

We often use abbreviations when writing short messages.

4 Match the highlighted colloquial expressions in the notes with the definitions below.
1 friends   4 very bad
2 come   5 a pity
3 receive a note, e-mail, etc. from you

5 Find one phrase from the *Learn this!* box on page 70 (Everyday English) in each note.

6 Imagine you are a friend of Mike's and have received his invitation. Plan two different notes: (a) declining the invitation, (b) accepting the invitation. Think about:
• what phrase you can use to accept/decline the invitation
• what reason you have for declining it (e.g. other plans)
• what questions you could ask when you accept the invitation

7 Write your two notes (50–70 words each). Use the plans below.
• Begin *Dear Mike* or *Hi Mike*
• Thank him for the invitation
• Decline the invitation
• Give your reason for declining it
• End with *Love* or *See you soon* and your name

• Begin *Dear Mike* or *Hi Mike*
• Thank him for the invitation
• Accept the invitation
• Ask a question about the occasion
• End with *Love* or *See you soon* and your name

Check your work

Have you
☐ used some colloquial expressions?
☐ used some abbreviations?
☐ written 50–70 words?
☐ checked your spelling, punctuation and grammar?

1 Read the texts quickly. Match the headings (1–3) with the texts (A–C).

1 The history of LEGO
2 The history of Monopoly
3 The history of the Razor Scooter

2 Do the Reading exam task.

READING exam task

Match the toys to sentences 1–9.
A = LEGO, B = Razor Scooter, C = Monopoly.

1 It took five years to develop.
2 Somebody designed it in the 1930s.
3 Its inventor used it in his factory.
4 Somebody who couldn't find a job developed it.
5 It wasn't very popular at first.
6 Three people developed it.
7 It immediately became popular in the country where it was invented.
8 Two people developed it.
9 It is a smaller version of a traditional toy.

A Ole Kirk Christiansen was a poor carpenter from Denmark who started a business making stepladders, ironing boards and wooden toys with his son Godtfred in 1932. The wooden toys quickly became the most popular product he sold, so in 1934 he decided to concentrate on making them and chose the name LEGO for their company. The word comes from two Danish words, 'LEg GOdt', meaning 'play well'. Coincidentally, in Latin *lego* means 'I put together'. In 1949, instead of the traditional wooden bricks, LEGO started making plastic building bricks which could be 'locked' together. However, at that time, plastic toys weren't very popular and the bricks were only sold in Denmark. In 1954 Christiansen's son, Godtfred, redesigned the bricks and global success followed.

B Gino Tsai was the owner of an enormous bicycle factory in Chang Hua, Taiwan. Tsai was a slow walker and didn't like walking around the factory. He tried riding a bicycle and a traditional scooter, but they were too big and awkward. So he spent five years developing a much smaller scooter that could be folded up. Tsai called it the 'Razor Scooter'. It is made of strong aluminum, which can support a 500 kg load without bending. In the late 1990s, it became a big hit in Japan and since then it has become popular all over the world as a quick, easy and fun way to get around.

C In the 1920s, Charles Darrow was a salesman in Pennsylvania, USA, but he lost his job in the Great Depression. He took various jobs to try to earn some money but none of them lasted long. One day he saw his neighbours playing a game in which the aim was to make money by buying and selling houses and hotels. Darrow decided to make a similar game and, with the help of his wife and son, developed a game called Monopoly. He took the game to Parker Brothers, a games manufacturer, who started to produce the game on a large scale. In its first year, 1935, it was America's best-selling game. Since then, over 500 million people have played Monopoly and it is now the most popular board game in the world.

3 Get ready to SPEAK Check the meaning of the domestic appliances in your dictionary. Then divide them into two groups and complete the table.

Domestic appliances dishwasher fridge freezer iron juicer kettle microwave oven toaster tumble dryer vacuum cleaner washing machine

For food and drink	For cleaning, washing and clothes
1	1
2	2
3	3
4	4
5	5
6	
7	

4 🎧 2.17 Listen to Laura and Robert arguing about which is the most useful appliance. Which appliances do they discuss? Which appliance do they decide is the most important?

5 🎧 2.17 Listen again and tick the expressions they use.

Agreeing
Yes, I agree (with you). That's true. That's right.
I couldn't agree more. I suppose you're right.

Disagreeing
I'm afraid I don't agree. I see what you mean, but …
I take your point, but … That may be true, but …
I'm not sure that's right.

6 Do the Speaking exam task.

SPEAKING exam task

Which are the two most important and useful appliances in exercise 3? Say why.

1 How often do you use them?
2 What do you use them for?
3 How can you do these tasks without the appliances?

1 Get ready to LISTEN **Ask and answer the questions.**

1 How often do you eat out?
2 What kind of restaurants do you like going to?
3 When you last ate out, who did you go with?
4 When you last ate out, what was the occasion?

2 Match 1–4 with a–d.

1	book	a	a dish
2	order	b	the bill
3	bring	c	a table
4	pay	d	the menu

3 Read the sentences in the listening task. Identify the part of speech of the missing words (e.g. noun, verb, adjective, etc.).

4 🎧 2.18 Do the Listening exam task.

LISTENING exam task

Listen to Thomas and Rachel talking about things going wrong at restaurants. Complete the sentences with the correct information. Write one word only in each gap.

Thomas' story
1 Christina's birthday was on _____.
2 Thomas' dad _____ him to the restaurant.
3 A _____ had to fix the car when it broke down.
4 Thomas forgot to bring Christina's present and _____.
5 Thomas couldn't pay his share of the _____.

Rachel's story
6 At first Rachel wanted to have a Chinese _____.
7 Rachel doesn't like _____ curries.
8 Rachel's dad _____ a table for eight o'clock.
9 Rachel realised what her dad's mistake was when she saw a _____.
10 The same _____ owns both restaurants.

5 Do the Use of English exam task.

USE OF ENGLISH exam task

Complete the text. Write one word only in each gap.

Jam Boy
Craig Flatman has an unusual diet. The 15-year-old boy has eaten only jam sandwiches [1]_____ eleven years. Craig is over six feet tall and keen [2]_____ sports, so it seems that the high-sugar diet has not affected his growth or energy levels. Dr David Rae carried out medical tests on Craig: the results were normal. Dr Rae, [3]_____ was a little surprised at the results, says Craig has [4]_____ eat more iron. Craig [5]_____ promised to improve his diet, but admits that the idea of eating fruit and vegetables makes [6]_____ sweat. Dr Rae thinks that if he continues to eat only jam sandwiches, his health will suffer in the future.

6 Get ready to SPEAK **Match the sentences 1–8 with the photos to give your opinion.**

Speculating
1 It looks *very cheap*.
2 It doesn't look *very lively*.
3 I should think that *the service is quite slow*.
4 It might be *quite expensive*.
5 It must be *very noisy*.
6 I don't expect that *the food is very good*.
7 I guess it's *quite formal*.
8 I expect that *the food is a bit basic*.

7 Do the Speaking exam task.

SPEAKING exam task

Compare and contrast the two photos. Which restaurant would you prefer to eat at? Give reasons. Think about these things:

1 the food
2 the cost
3 the atmosphere
4 the service

8 What if ...?

THIS UNIT INCLUDES ●●●●○
Vocabulary • global issues • word formation: noun suffixes
Grammar • second conditional • *I wish ...*
Speaking • discussing global issues • giving advice
Writing • an essay

A VOCABULARY AND LISTENING
Global issues

I can talk about global problems.

1 Read the speaking tip below and look at photo 1. Which words from the box do you need to describe it?

> cold   dangerous   gun   home   poor   sleep
> sleeping bag   smoke   street

Speaking tip

Look at the photo closely before you answer. Think what English words you will need to describe it.

2 SPEAKING Answer the questions about photo 1. Use the words in exercise 1 to help you.

1 Where is he?
2 Why is he there?
3 What's he doing?
4 How do you think he's feeling?

3 Match the photos 1–6 with words from the box.

> Global issues   the arms trade   child labour   disease
> endangered species   famine   global warming   war
> homelessness   pollution   poverty   racism   terrorism

4 🎧 2.19 Listen and repeat all the words. Check the meanings in your dictionary.

> ●●●●● Vocabulary Builder (part 1): page 131

5 🎧 2.20 Listen to the radio programmes. Which issues in exercise 3 are the six people talking about?

Speaker 1	Speaker 2	Speaker 3

Speaker 4	Speaker 5	Speaker 6

6 SPEAKING Work in pairs. Which three issues in exercise 3 do you think are the most serious for (a) your country? (b) the world?

> We think the three most serious issues for our country are ...

> We think the three most serious issues for the world are ...

> ●●●●● Vocabulary Builder (part 2): page 131

Second conditional

I can talk about an imaginary situation and its consequences.

1 🎧 **2.21** Listen and complete the text with the words in the box. Why is vegetable oil better than petrol?

| had   used   wouldn't produce   would earn |

Darryl Hannah is a Hollywood star who cares about the environment. Her car is very unusual because it doesn't use petrol – it uses vegetable oil, which produces very little CO_2. 'If all our cars [1]_____ it, we [2]_____ so much CO_2. It's also renewable – we can grow it. If more people [3]_____ cars like mine, the world's farmers [4]_____ more money.'

LEARN THIS!

1 We use the **second conditional** to describe an imaginary situation or event, and its result.

2 We use the past tense in the *if* clause, and *would/wouldn't* + verb in the main clause.

If all our cars used vegetable oil, we wouldn't produce so much CO_2.

↑ imaginary situation/event   ↑ result

3 In the *if* clause, we can use *were* instead of *was* as the past tense of *be*, singular.

If the weather were nicer, I'd go out.

2 Study the information in the *Learn this!* box. Complete the text with *would* and verbs from the box below. You will have to use some of the verbs more than once.

| be   consume   earn   own   speak   not be   not have |

There are 6.3 billion people in the world. Numbers as big as this are difficult to understand. However, if the world were a village of 100 people, …

- 61 [would be] Asian and 12 _____ European.
- 22 _____ Chinese and 9 _____ English.
- 20 _____ less than $1 a day.
- 24 _____ any electricity in their home.
- 7 _____ a car.
- 20 _____ 80% of the energy.
- 67 _____ able to read.

Grammar Builder (8B): page 118

3 Match the halves of the sentences. Complete them with the correct form of the verbs in brackets.

1 If we _____ (not produce) so much CO_2,
2 I _____ (give) a lot of money to charity
3 We _____ (save) millions of lives
4 The world _____ (be) a safer place
5 If we _____ (not pollute) our rivers,

a if scientists _____ (be able to) stop diseases like AIDS.
b they _____ (be) full of fish.
c we _____ (reduce) global warming.
d if I _____ (be) very rich.
e if we _____ (stop) the arms trade.

4 Complete the sentences with the correct form of the verbs in brackets.

If we [1]_____ (recycle) more plastic bottles, we [2]_____ (not have to) produce so much plastic.

If we [3]_____ (produce) less plastic, we [4]_____ (burn) less oil.

If we [5]_____ (burn) less oil, there [6]_____ (not be) so many 'greenhouse gases' in the atmosphere.

If there [7]_____ (not be) so many greenhouse gases in the atmosphere, we [8]_____ (be able to) reduce global warming.

If we [9]_____ (reduce) global warming, the Earth's climate [10]_____ (not change) so fast.

5 **SPEAKING** Work in pairs. What would you do in these situations? Make notes. Ask and answer the questions.

> What would you do if you found 100 euros in the street?

> Where would you live if you could live anywhere in the world?

1 If you found 100 euros in the street …
2 If you could live anywhere in the world …
3 If you saw someone attacking an old man in the street …
4 If you didn't have to go to school …
5 If you could choose any job you wanted …
6 If you borrowed a friend's MP3 player and accidentally broke it …
7 If you saw someone in your class cheating in an exam …

6 **SPEAKING** Tell the class about your partner.

> If Dannie found 100 euros in the street, she'd …

I can talk about the environment.

1 🎧 2.22 Do the environment quiz. Listen and check your answers.

Environment Quiz

1 How long does it take a plastic bag to decompose?
a up to 10 years   b up to 100 years   c up to 1,000 years

2 The ozone layer
a stops ultra-violet light from the sun.
b causes global warming.
c is pollution in the atmosphere.

3 How much of our energy comes from oil, coal and gas?
a 30%   b 60%   c 90%

4 On average, how much rubbish do EU countries recycle?
a 35%   b 45%   c 65%

5 In which of these foods has the British government found a lot of pesticides?
a baby food   b bread   c chips   d all of these

2 🎧 2.22 Listen again. Answer the questions.

1 What should we do when we go shopping?
2 How high above the surface of the Earth is the ozone layer?
3 When we burn oil, coal and gas, what problem does it cause?
4 How much rubbish does the EU want to recycle?
5 How many pesticides are regularly used in non-organic farming?

3 Complete the text with the words in the box.

countries   energy   environment
letters   rubbish   turn off   use

PRO EUROPE

Youth eco-Parliament

Teen action!

In 2004, 120 young people between the ages of fourteen and seventeen from ten European ¹_____ met in Berlin at the first Youth Eco-Parliament. Before going to Berlin, they made plans for improving the ²_____ in their own towns and villages. They focused on areas like recycling, saving ³_____, and reducing pollution. After that they went to Berlin and discussed their plans. Then they wrote ⁴_____ giving ideas for improving the environment, locally, nationally and globally. Here are some of the things they think we should do:

1 recycle more ⁵_____ (for example, glass, paper, plastic, metal)

2 use our cars less – use public transport and bikes, or walk

3 stop polluting rivers and streams

4 pick up rubbish in parks and in the street

5 save energy – ⁶_____ lights and TVs when we're not using them

6 don't use too many pesticides on farms

7 use recycled paper

8 ⁷_____ shopping bags instead of plastic bags

The Youth Eco-Parliament is going to meet every two years. To find out more about it, visit their website: www.eyep.info/

4 SPEAKING Work in small groups. Talk about how people could improve the environment in your village, town or country. Use ideas in the text to help you.

> If people didn't drop litter, the streets would be cleaner.

5 Write an open e-mail to people telling them how to improve the environment in your town or village. Use your ideas from exercise 4.

Dear Friend,

If you care about the environment, you'll want to do everything you can to improve it. Here are some practical ideas.
● Try to …
● Don't …
● If we …

8D GRAMMAR
I wish ...

I can talk about situations I would like to change.

1 Look at the cartoons. Answer the questions.

> I wish I didn't have so much homework.

1 Does the boy have a lot of homework?

> I wish I could fly.

2 Can the cat fly?

> DEAR DAVID, I WISH YOU WERE HERE

3 Is the girl's boyfriend there?

2 Which tense do we use after *wish*? Study the information in the *Learn this!* box. Choose the correct tense to complete the rule.

> **LEARN THIS!**
>
> **1** We use *wish* + the **present / past / future** to say that we want something to be different from how it is now.
> *I wish I could play the piano.*
> *Do you ever wish you had a lot of money?*
> *I wish it wasn't raining.*
>
> **2** We can use *were* instead of *was* after *I*, *he*, *she* and *it*.
> *I wish I were 21.*

🔘●●●● Grammar Builder (8D): page 118

3 Write sentences starting with *I wish*.

1 I can't drive.
   I wish I could drive.
2 I don't have a dog.
3 I don't like vegetables.
4 I'm not very good at maths.
5 I don't speak French.
6 I can't play the guitar.
7 I've got a lot of homework.
8 I'm not very tall.

4 🎧 2.23 Listen and complete the song with the phrases in the box.

> be like a bird   break all the chains   break all the chains
> know how it feels   say all the things   say all the things
> share all the love   soar to the sun

(I Wish I Knew How It Would Feel To Be) Free

I wish I knew how it would feel to be free
I wish I could [1]_____ holding me
I wish I could [2]_____ that I should say
Say them loud say them clear
For the whole wide world to hear

I wish I could [3]_____ that's in my heart
Remove all the bars that keep us apart
And I wish you could [4]_____ to be me
Then you'd see and agree that every man should be free

I wish I could [5]_____ in the sky
How sweet it would be if I found I could fly
Well I'd [6]_____ and look down at the sea
And I'd sing cos I'd know how it feels to be free

I wish I knew how it would feel to be free
I wish I could [7]_____ holding me
And I wish I could [8]_____ that I wanna say
Say them loud say them clear
For the whole wide world to hear
Say them loud say them clear
For the whole wide world to hear
Say them loud say them clear
For the whole wide world to hear

> **Glossary**
> soar = fly
> cos = because
> wanna = want to

5 Complete the sentences with your own ideas.

1 I wish I were ...
2 I wish I weren't ...
3 I wish I had ...
4 I wish I lived ...
5 I wish I knew ...
6 I wish I could ...
7 I wish I spoke ...

6 **SPEAKING** Work in pairs. Compare your wishes with your partner.

1 Work in pairs. Match the countries with the volcanoes. Can you name any other volcanoes?

Indonesia	Italy	Japan	Mexico

1 Mount Fuji (last eruption: 1707)
2 Vesuvius (last eruption: 1944)
3 Krakatoa (last eruption: 2001)
4 Popocatepetl (last eruption: 2006)

> *Tip*
>
> If the text includes a diagram, look at it closely before you read. If you understand the diagram, it will be easier to understand the text.

2 Read the text quickly. Are the sentences true or false?

1 The volcano is in Africa.
2 The volcano could cause a tsunami.
3 We can prevent the eruption of the volcano.

3 Read the text again. What do the numbers refer to?

1 6
2 500 billion
3 800
4 90
5 8

4 Answer the questions.

1 Why are scientists worried about Cumbre Vieja?
2 How long would it take the wave to reach the African coast?
3 Why would Europe be in less danger than America?
4 How big would the wave be when it reached Portugal?
5 Why would it travel a long way inland in the Caribbean and South America?
6 What can scientists do to predict the eruptions?

5 Find these highlighted words in the text.

1 two adjectives that mean 'very big'
2 two verbs that mean 'damage very badly'

6 Find the highlighted verbs in the text that belong to the same word family as the nouns.

1 destruction
2 devastation
3 eruption
4 prediction
5 protection

7 **SPEAKING** Read the text again. Cover the text, and say what would happen if the volcano collapsed. Use the words in the box to help you.

Nouns side volcano tonnes of rock sea tsunami Atlantic Ocean coast wave
Verbs collapse cause travel across reach destroy

> If the volcano collapsed, tonnes of rock would fall into the sea.

WAVE POWER

This is a picture of Cumbre Vieja, a huge, active volcano on La Palma in the Canary Islands. Every few decades it erupts, and scientists are worried because the walls of the volcano are getting weaker. Scientists fear that when it erupts, one side of the volcano could collapse and fall into the sea. If this happened, it would be a catastrophe. Why? Because it would cause a tsunami – an enormous wave – the biggest ever recorded in history.

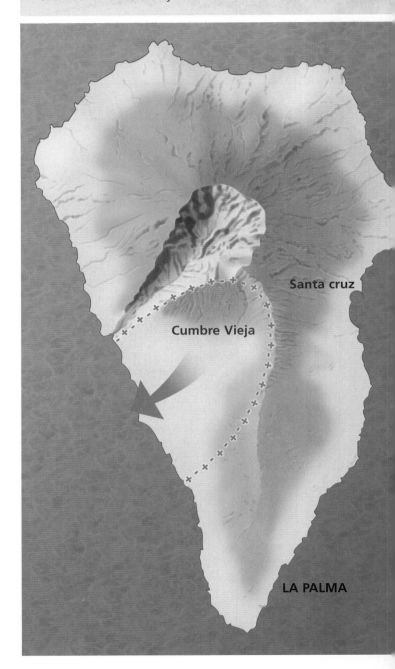

Santa cruz

Cumbre Vieja

LA PALMA

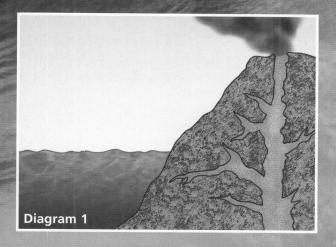

Diagram 1

Diagram 2

How would it happen?

The volcano is by the sea, and the water next to the volcano is about six kilometres deep. If the volcano collapsed, 500 billion tonnes of rock would fall into the sea. This would create a huge tsunami about 100 metres high (see Diagrams 1 and 2).

What would happen next?

The wave would travel away from the Canary Islands in all directions at about 800 km/h. The other Canary Islands would immediately be covered by water. In less than an hour a 90-metre wave would hit north-west Africa. The side of the volcano faces west, across the Atlantic Ocean, which would protect Europe a little. However, a 12-metre tsunami would still reach Lisbon within three hours. After five hours it would reach Britain. The wave could travel a kilometre inland, and devastate towns and villages. London would be flooded. (See map.)

How far would it travel?

The wave would have enough energy to travel right across the Atlantic Ocean. Eight hours after the eruption it would hit the east coast of America. It would still be about 30 metres high. Boston would be hit first, followed by New York, then the coast down to Miami. The wave would cause a lot of damage in the Caribbean and Brazil too. It would travel for several kilometres inland because the coast is very flat. It would destroy everything and kill thousands of people.

What can we do about it?

Nothing much, it seems. The scientists believe that it is not a question of if, but when. The volcano will collapse at some time in the future, but it could be hundreds or thousands of years from now. Furthermore, if only part of the volcano collapsed into the sea, the tsunami would be much smaller. Scientists want to put better equipment on Cumbre Vieja, so that they can predict the volcano's eruptions in the future and give us an early warning of possible problems.

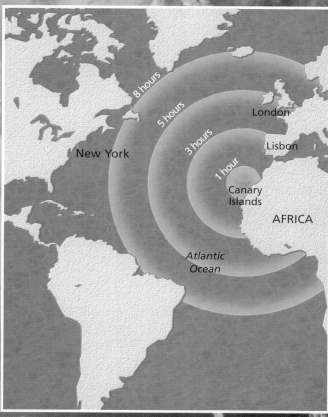

Giving advice

I can describe a problem and give advice.

1 🎧 2.24 Complete the dialogue with the words in the box. Then listen and check.

> advice   borrowed   idea   lent   upset

Mark	Can I ask your ¹_____ about something?
Lucy	Sure. What's the problem?
Mark	I ²_____ £20 to Joe last week and he hasn't paid me back. I think he's forgotten about it.
Lucy	I think you should ask him to pay you back.
Mark	Yes, but it's embarrassing. He might get ³_____ .
Lucy	If I were you, I'd say, 'I'm a bit short of money, Joe. When do you think you could pay back the £20 you ⁴_____ last week?' He shouldn't get upset at that.
Mark	OK. Thanks. That's a good ⁵_____ .

LEARN THIS!

1 We use *should* and ***ought to*** for suggestions, advice and opinions.

2 We often use *I think* or *I don't think* with ***should*** and ***ought to***.
I think you ought to go to bed.
I don't think you should stay up late.

2 SPEAKING Work in pairs. Practise reading the dialogue.

3 What do you think of the advice that Lucy gives? Would you give different advice?

I wouldn't tell Mark to ... / I'd tell him to ...

Exam tip

Don't worry if you don't understand every word in the recording on the first listening. Try to understand the general sense of it.

4 🎧 2.25 Listen to the conversation. What is Will's problem?

5 🎧 2.25 Listen again. Are the sentences true or false?

1 Will arrived home very late one day last week.
2 Will's parents were cross because he missed the bus.
3 Will didn't apologise because he wasn't sorry.
4 Sally thinks Will should apologise for being late.

6 🎧 2.26 PRONUNCIATION Listen and repeat the phrases in the box. Pay attention to how *should/shouldn't*, *would/wouldn't* are pronounced.

> **Giving advice**   I think you should ...
> I think you ought to ...   If I were you, I would ...
> If I were you, I wouldn't ...   Why don't you ...?
> I don't think you should ...   I don't think you ought to ...
> In my opinion, you shouldn't ...

7 Write advice for the problems. Start with phrases from exercise 6 and include the words in brackets.

1 'I'm really tired.' (go to bed)
  If I were you, I would go to bed.
2 'I've got a difficult exam tomorrow.' (revise)
3 'This milk smells bad.' (drink it)
4 'I really like a girl in my class.' (tell her)
5 'I've got sun burn.' (sit in the sun)
6 'I've lost my brother's sunglasses.' (buy him some new ones)

8 SPEAKING Work in pairs. Choose one of the problems below, or invent one of your own. Talk about what advice you would give.

Problems & Possible advice

1 My girlfriend/boyfriend has given me a T-shirt for my birthday, but I hate it.
* Don't tell him/her that you don't like it. Wear it anyway.
* Tell him/her you don't like it. Ask if you can take it back to the shop and change it.

2 There's a boy/girl in my class that I really like but I'm not sure if he/she likes me, so I'm afraid to ask him/her out.
* Go and talk to him/her. Just relax, smile and be friendly.
* Don't speak to him/her. It might be embarrassing.

3 My friend Tessa is going out with a boy called Wayne. But I saw Wayne with another girl at the cinema last night.
* Tell Tessa that you saw Wayne with another girl.
* Ask Tessa if she's happy with Wayne, but don't tell her that you saw Wayne with another girl.

9 SPEAKING Work in pairs. Now write a dialogue about the problem and advice you talked about in exercise 8. Use the phrases for giving advice from exercise 6. Then practise reading your dialogue in pairs.

10 SPEAKING Act out your dialogues to the class. Does the class agree with the advice you gave each other?

1 Read Cathy's essay. Which global issues does she mention?

- ☐ the arms trade
- ☐ disease
- ☐ homelessness
- ☐ endangered species
- ☐ famine
- ☐ racism
- ☐ global warming
- ☐ terrorism

If I ruled the world   **by Cathy**

If I ruled the world, the first thing I'd do is prevent famine and disease in the developing world. In my opinion, that's one of the most serious problems we face. I'd make sure that poor farmers could sell their food to the rest of the world. I'd also make more medicines available to people in poor countries. I believe we could save millions of lives by vaccinating children, so I'd make drugs companies do that.

The next thing I'd do is make governments invest in wind, water and solar power. In my view, we need to stop global warming, so I'd also make petrol-driven cars illegal.

There are some less serious things I'd do too. I'd ban rap music because I think it's terrible and I'd reduce the number of sports programmes on television. Finally, I'd make my brother change his socks every day because they smell awful.

2 Answer the questions.

1 How would Cathy help farmers in the developing world?
2 What would she make drugs companies do?
3 Why would she make petrol-driven cars illegal?
4 What would she ban?
5 What kind of TV programme doesn't she like?
6 What would she make her brother do?

3 Read the writing tip. How many of the phrases can you find in the essay? Underline them. Translate all the phrases.

> ### Writing tip
>
> We can use these phrases for expressing opinions:
>
> | | |
> |---|---|
> | *I think (that) …* | *I don't think (that) …* |
> | *I believe (that) …* | *I don't believe (that) …* |
> | *In my view, …* | *In my opinion, …* |
> | *I'm convinced that …* | *As I see it, …* |

4 Find examples of these structures in the essay.

1 make somebody do something
2 make somebody/something + adjective
3 make sure that …

5 Complete the sentences with the verbs and adjectives in the box.

> found   illegal   optional   pick up   reduce
> smaller   stop   was

1 I'd make all drugs _____ .
2 I'd make sure that the government _____ a home for every homeless person.
3 I'd make factories _____ the amount of pollution they produce.
4 I'd make cars _____ and cleaner.
5 I'd make people _____ their own litter.
6 I'd make sure that clean water _____ available to everyone in the world.
7 I'd make school _____ instead of compulsory.
8 I'd make smokers _____ smoking.

6 Do this writing task. Include some serious and some less serious ideas, and use some of the phrases and structures in exercises 3 and 4. Follow the writing plan below.

> **Write an essay about what you'd do if you ruled the world. Write 130–150 words.**
>
> - The first thing I'd do is …
> - I'd also …
> - The next thing I'd do is …
> - There are some less serious things I'd do too.
> - Finally, I'd …

> ### Check your work
>
> **Have you**
>
> - ☐ divided your essay into paragraphs?
> - ☐ used phrases for expressing opinions?
> - ☐ used expressions with *make* correctly?
> - ☐ written 130–150 words?
> - ☐ checked your spelling, punctuation and grammar?

Vocabulary

1 Complete the expressions with the words in the box.

| arms back hands head legs |

1 cross your _____
2 fold your _____
3 hold _____
4 shake your _____
5 pat somebody on the _____

Mark /5

2 Match the slogans with the global issues in the box.

| child labour   disease   endangered species   famine
global warming   homelessness   pollution   racism |

1 Everybody needs a home.
2 Black and white people are equal.
3 Children need education, not jobs.
4 Factories are destroying our environment.
5 The climate is changing.
6 Save the tiger.
7 Malaria kills millions of children every year.
8 People are dying because there isn't any food.

Mark /8

Grammar

3 Choose the correct word.

1 You **must / mustn't / needn't** have tea. There's coffee too.
2 You **must / mustn't / needn't** swim in the sea today. There are sharks!
3 You **must / mustn't / needn't** wear a suit to the wedding. You can wear casual clothes, if you prefer.
4 You **must / mustn't / needn't** use a knife and fork. It's rude to eat with your fingers.
5 You **must / mustn't / needn't** turn off your mobile in class.
6 You **must / mustn't / needn't** use a mobile phone on a plane. It's dangerous.

Mark /6

4 Match the two halves of the first conditional sentences and complete them.

1 You _____ (not pass) your exam
2 We _____ (not have) a barbecue
3 If he _____ (invite) me to the party,
4 If they _____ (leave) now,
5 I _____ (not be) angry
6 If I _____ (buy) a new MP3 player,

a I _____ (accept).
b they _____ (get) home before eight o'clock.
c if you _____ (not study).
d I _____ (give) you my old one.
e if you _____ (forget) my birthday.
f if it _____ (rain).

Mark /6

5 Complete the second conditional sentences.

1 If I _____ (have) the money, I _____ (buy) a new phone.
2 She _____ (have) friends if she _____ (not be) so rude.
3 You _____ (be) healthier if you _____ (do) more exercise.
4 I _____ (not do) that if I _____ (be) you.
5 If they _____ (speak) Italian, they _____ (be able to) ask for directions.
6 If you _____ (not be) so slow, I _____ (not get) so impatient!

Mark /6

6 Write sentences with *I wish ... .*

1 Oh no! It's raining!
  I wish it wasn't raining.
2 Oh no! The supermarket is shut!
3 Oh no! I haven't got my mobile phone!
4 Oh no! My homework is really difficult!
5 Oh no! I can't find my bag!
6 Oh no! It's Monday!
7 Oh no! We've got an exam tomorrow!

Mark /6

Everyday English

7 Complete the dialogue with the questions.

a Do you like pizza?
b Shall I bring some food?
c Shall I eat before I come?
d Would you like to come?
e What time?

Bob   I'm going to the cinema tomorrow. [1] _____
Jenny I'd love to, thanks. [2] _____
Bob   About seven o'clock.
Jenny [3] _____
Bob   No, we're going to eat at my house before the film.
Jenny [4] _____
Bob   No, it's OK. I've got some pizzas at home. [5] _____
Jenny Yes, I love it!

Mark /5

8 Complete the dialogue with the words in the box.

| advice   afford   borrow   course   problem   should
understand   were |

Boy   Can I ask your [1] _____ about something?
Girl Yes, of [2] _____. What's the [3] _____?
Boy   It's my friend's birthday tomorrow, but I can't [4] _____ to buy him a present.
Girl If I [5] _____ you, I'd just get him a nice card.
Boy   Really? I could [6] _____ some money from my parents.
Girl I don't think you [7] _____ do that. If you explain to your friend that you haven't got any money, he'll [8] _____.

Mark /8

TOTAL /50

Listening

1 🎧 **2.27** **Listen to the conversations. Which problem does Joanna have at the end?**

1 She wants to go to the Notting Hill Carnival but Daniel doesn't want to go.
2 She wants to go to Daniel's barbecue but she's already arranged to go to the carnival with the family.
3 She hasn't seen Daniel for a long time but is afraid to ask him to the carnival.

2 🎧 **2.27** **Listen again. Are the sentences true or false?**

1 Joanna went to the cinema with Daniel on Saturday.
2 It's the Notting Hill Carnival next Sunday.
3 Joanna usually works at weekends.
4 Joanna invites Daniel to the barbecue.
5 Daniel's barbecue starts at one o'clock.
6 Daniel wants Joanna to bring some food.

Speaking

3 **Work in pairs. Imagine you are Joanna and a friend. Prepare a dialogue using Joanna's problem from exercise 1 and the plan below.**

Joanna	Friend
Ask for some advice.	
	Ask what the problem is.
Tell your friend the problem.	
	Say what you think Joanna should do.
Agree. Thank your friend for the advice.	

4 **Act out your dialogue to the class.**

Reading

5 **Describe the photo below and the photo on the right. Answer the questions. Use the words in the box to help you.**

> **Nouns** T-shirt sunglasses costume drums
> **Verbs** play dance sing laugh
> **Adjectives** colourful excited happy nervous

1 What are the people wearing? What are they doing?
2 How do you think the people are feeling?

6 **Read the text below. Match each paragraph with one of the following headings. There is one extra heading that you don't need.**

a Problems at the carnival
b Famous people at the carnival
c The history of the carnival
d The main events at the carnival

7 **Answer the questions.**

1 When does the carnival take place?
2 What happens on the first day of the carnival?
3 Who started the carnival?
4 What changed in 1965?
5 How many spectators were there in 2000?
6 Why are the narrow streets in Notting Hill a problem?

Writing

8 **Think of a festival or special event in your country. Write a note to your partner inviting him or her to it.**

9 **Work in pairs. Exchange invitations with your partner, then write a reply. Student A: Accept the invitation. Student B: Decline the invitation.**

1 The Notting Hill Carnival is the largest street festival in Europe. It takes place in Notting Hill, an area of London, every year in August and it lasts for three days. On Saturday, the first day, there is a competition between groups of musicians who play special metal drums called 'steel drums'. Sunday is children's day and there is a special parade for children and young people. The main parade is on Monday.

2 The carnival began in 1959. It was the idea of members of the Caribbean community who lived there. At first, it was an indoor event, but in 1965 it moved outdoors. At this time, only about 1,000 people went to the carnival each year, but the numbers soon started to grow. By 2000, there were about 1.5 million spectators!

3 In the past, there has been some trouble at the carnival, especially between spectators and the police. And there have also been worries about safety because the crowds are large and the streets are narrow. For these reasons, some people have suggested banning the carnival. However, it is now an important event in London – not just for the Caribbean community there, but for the whole capital.

9 Crime scene

THIS UNIT INCLUDES ●●●●●○
Vocabulary • crimes and criminals • crime verbs • extreme adjectives • word formation: noun suffixes -er, -ist and -ian • colloquial expressions
Grammar • past perfect • reported speech
Speaking • asking and replying to personal questions • reporting a theft • giving opinions
Writing • a story

A · VOCABULARY AND LISTENING
Crimes and criminals

I can describe different crimes.

1 Look at the photos. Can you name any of the crimes?

2 Match the extracts from the newspaper reports with the photos.

a Joyriders stole four cars in Oxford last night …

b The police are questioning a group of vandals who smashed bus shelters in the town centre …

c A shoplifter stole an MP3 player from a department store …

d Last year drug dealers sold £1 million of heroin and cocaine on the streets of Manchester …

e Police arrested a burglar who broke into three houses on Friday evening …

f Robbers robbed a bank in Liverpool yesterday morning. They took £1,000,000 …

3 Are any of these crimes a problem where you live?

4 Complete the table with the words in the box. Which two crimes aren't in the photos above?

Crimes	burglary	joyriding	murder	robbery	sell
steal	theft	vandalise			

Crime	Criminal	Verb
¹ _____	burglar	burgle a house
drug dealing	drug dealer	² _____ drugs
³ _____	joyrider	go joyriding
murder	murderer	⁴ _____ someone
⁵ _____	robber	rob someone/a bank, shop, etc.
shoplifting	shoplifter	⁶ _____ something from a shop
⁷ _____	thief	steal something
vandalism	vandal	⁸ _____ something

5 🎧 2.29 Listen and check.

Look out! *rob* and *steal*
You *rob* a place or a person.
Two men robbed a bank yesterday.
You *steal* something from a person or a place.
Thieves stole jewellery from the shop.

●●●● Vocabulary Builder (part 1): page 132

6 🎧 2.30 Listen to the dialogues. Which crimes are the people talking about? Choose the correct answers.

1 **a** burglary   **b** vandalism
2 **a** robbery   **b** shoplifting
3 **a** drug dealing   **b** theft
4 **a** robbery   **b** shoplifting
5 **a** joyriding   **b** theft

7 SPEAKING Work in pairs. Decide which three of the crimes in exercise 4 are the most serious, and why. Make notes.

8 SPEAKING Tell the class which crimes you have chosen, and why.

We think ____ is the most serious crime because …

●●●● Vocabulary Builder (part 1): page 132

9B GRAMMAR
Past perfect

I can describe an event using different past tenses.

1 Read the text. Why was the man stupid?

Listeners to a radio programme in Chicago were very surprised when a man phoned the programme and said that he was a bank robber. At the beginning of the programme, the presenter **had asked** listeners to call in and confess to any 'small crimes' they **had committed**.

The man described the crime exactly. Five months earlier, he and four other men **had gone** to a bank in Chicago and **had stolen** $81,000. A woman who worked in the bank **had** also **helped** in the robbery. The man was obviously very proud of himself. He didn't give his name on the radio, but police later discovered the man's telephone number and arrested him.

2 Look at the verbs in blue in the text. Did these events happen *before* or *after* the man called the radio station?

3 Complete the rule in the *Learn this!* box with *before*, *after* or *at the same time as*.

> **LEARN THIS!**
> 1 We form the **past perfect** with *had* or *hadn't* + past participle.
> 2 We use the **past perfect** to talk about an event that happened _____ another event in the past.
> *When the police arrived at the house, the burglar had escaped.*
> *I was sure I hadn't met him before.*
> *Had she already left the house when you phoned?*

●●●●● Grammar Builder (9B): page 120

4 **SPEAKING** Work in pairs. By the time you arrived at school this morning, which of these things had you done? Ask and answer the questions using the past perfect.

> Had you had a shower?

> Yes, I had. / No, I hadn't.

1 have a shower
2 have breakfast
3 watch TV
4 finish all your homework
5 send an e-mail
6 make a phone call

5 Complete the text with the past perfect form of the verbs in brackets.

YESTERDAY afternoon Australian police chased two joyriders in a stolen car for 600 kilometres. Earlier in the day, the joyriders ¹_____ (steal) a car in Adelaide and ²_____ then _____ (stop) for petrol at Wirulla. But they ³_____ (not pay for) the petrol and the owner of the petrol station called the police. The police chased the stolen car but it was too fast for them. They eventually caught up with it three hours later. The joyriders ⁴_____ (run out of) fuel. Earlier, the police ⁵_____ (realise) that they couldn't keep up with the stolen car, so they ⁶_____ (order) all petrol stations in the area to close!

6 Complete the sentences. Use the past perfect and your own ideas.

1 I was upset because I had failed the exam.
2 I felt really happy because …
3 I suddenly realised that …
4 I was angry because …
5 I forgot that …

7 Imagine one bad thing that happened yesterday, and write it down. Look at the examples to help you.

- Somebody stole my bike.
- My sister broke my computer.
- The dog was sick in my trainers.

8 **SPEAKING** Memory Game! Take it in turns around the class to repeat the whole sentence and add your idea from exercise 7. Remember to use the past perfect.

> When I got home yesterday, somebody had stolen my bike.

> When I got home yesterday, somebody had stolen my bike, and my sister had broken my computer.

> When I got home yesterday, somebody had stolen my bike, my sister had broken my computer, and the dog had been sick in my trainers.

1 Look at the picture. Do you know the detective on the right? Describe him. Was he a real character or was he fictional?

Elementary, my dear Watson!

DETECTIVE STORIES are the most popular type of stories in the world. But who is the most famous fictional detective? Without a doubt, it is Sherlock Holmes.

The author of the Sherlock Holmes stories was Arthur Conan Doyle. He was born in Scotland in 1859 and studied medicine at Edinburgh university. After leaving university he moved to the south of England and worked as a doctor, but in his spare time he started to write detective stories.

The hero of the stories is a private detective called Sherlock Holmes, who lives at 221b Baker Street in London. There is now a museum at that address. (See http://www.sherlock-holmes.co.uk.) Holmes is tall and thin, with a long, sharp face. He usually wears a deerstalker hat, smokes a pipe or cigarettes, and carries a magnifying glass. He is an extremely intelligent man who always thinks logically about the crimes he is trying to solve. He is also a brilliant violinist. However, he has a dark side to his character: he is a lonely and rather sad man who is easily bored with everyday life. He often gets depressed and sometimes spends all day in bed. He is not married and says that he doesn't understand women. Holmes lives with his assistant and only friend, Dr Watson. Watson describes him in one of the stories as 'a brain without a heart' and 'more a machine than a man'.

In 1895, after Conan Doyle had written 25 stories about Holmes, he got bored with his detective and decided that Holmes would die in the next story. At the end of the story called *The Final Problem*, Holmes fights Professor Moriarty, his greatest enemy, by a huge waterfall in Switzerland. They both die when they fall into the waterfall. But the Holmes stories were already incredibly popular and his fans were very upset. Conan Doyle had to bring his character back to life. He continued to write Sherlock Holmes stories for another 25 years. In the end, he wrote four novels and 56 short stories about the great detective.

2 Read the text. Which one of the descriptions of Holmes is not completely accurate?

1 A very intelligent man who didn't have many friends and didn't understand women.
2 A sad and lonely man who easily got depressed and sometimes spent all day in bed.
3 A brilliant logical thinker who lived with his assistant Dr Watson and never got married.
4 An intelligent, funny, friendly man who smoked a pipe and played the violin brilliantly.

3 Are the sentences true or false?

1 Arthur Conan Doyle was Scottish.
2 By 1895 Conan Doyle had written all his Sherlock Holmes stories.
3 Conan Doyle wrote the Sherlock Holmes stories in Scotland.
4 Holmes dies at the end of *The Final Problem*.
5 Conan Doyle started to write about Holmes again because his fans were very unhappy.
6 In total, Conan Doyle wrote 25 stories and four novels about Holmes.

4 🎧 2.31 Listen to part one of a Sherlock Holmes story called *The Speckled Band*. Put the events of Helen Stoner's life in the correct order.

☐ Her mother marries Doctor Roylott.
☐ Doctor Roylott murders a servant.
☐ The family returns to England.
☐ Her father dies.
☐ Helen's mother dies.
☐ Somebody burgles their house in India.
☐ Doctor Roylott goes to prison.
☐ Helen's twin sister, Julia, dies in her bedroom.

Exam tip

Read the list of events and make sure you understand everything before you listen to the recording. Use logic to do the task. For example, do people go to prison *before* or *after* they have committed a crime?

5 🎧 2.32 Listen to part two of the story. Answer the questions.

1 How did Julia Stoner die?
2 What happens to Doctor Roylott?

6 **SPEAKING** Ask and answer the questions.

1 Have you seen any Sherlock Holmes films or read any of the stories? If so, did you enjoy them?
2 How many books, films or TV shows about crime and detectives can you name?
3 How do crime stories usually begin? How do they usually end?
4 Do you enjoy reading or watching crime stories? Why?/Why not?

Reported speech

I can report what other people have said.

1 Read the text. Was the bank robber successful?

Crime doesn't pay

A man walked into the Bank of America and wrote on a bank form, 'This is a robery. Put all yur munney in this bag.' Then he waited in the queue. But he was worried that someone had seen him write the note, so he left the Bank of America and crossed the street to the Wells Fargo Bank. He gave the note to a bank assistant there, and said that he was robbing the bank. The assistant read the note. She noticed his spelling mistakes, and decided that he wasn't very clever. She said that he was in the Wells Fargo Bank and said that he needed to take the form to the Bank of America. The man looked upset, but he left the Wells Fargo Bank. The assistant then quickly called the police. She told the police that a man had tried to rob the bank. The police arrested the man a few minutes later. He was waiting in the queue at the Bank of America.

2 Read the quotations and decide who said them. Underline the parts of the text that give you the answers.

1 'I'm robbing the bank.'
2 'You are in the Wells Fargo Bank.'
3 'You need to take the form to the Bank of America.'
4 'A man tried to rob the bank.'

3 Compare the quotations in exercise 2 with the parts of the text that you underlined. How do the verbs and pronouns change? Look at the information in the *Learn this!* box and complete the rules.

LEARN THIS!

When you change **direct speech** to **reported speech**
1 verbs in the present simple usually change to
  a the future.
  b the past simple.
2 verbs in the present continuous usually change to
  a the present simple.
  b the past continuous.
3 verbs in the past simple usually change to
  a the past perfect.
  b the present perfect.
4 pronouns
  a always change.
  b sometimes change, depending on the context.

4 Rewrite the quotations in reported speech. Change the pronouns if necessary.

1 'I want to catch the thief,' the policeman said.
  The policeman said that he wanted to catch the thief.
2 'She stole a CD from the music shop,' he said.
3 'The police arrested a drug dealer,' she said.
4 'I go joyriding at weekends,' he said.
5 'We are questioning two teenagers about the burglary,' the policeman said.
6 'A boy in my class vandalised a phone box,' my sister said.
7 'Jake is a drug dealer,' said Mark.
8 'The police are looking for the bank robbers,' she said.

●○○● Grammar Builder (9D): page 120

5 Write down three short sentences using the present simple, present continuous and past simple.

I like Anastacia.
It isn't raining.
I went to the cinema last night.

6 **SPEAKING** Work in pairs. Read the sentences to your partner. Your partner reports them to the class.

I like Anastacia.

James said that he liked Anastacia.

7 Underline the reported speech in the text. Change it to direct speech.

An old lady had spent the morning with a friend at a shopping centre in Los Angeles. When they returned to the car, they found four men sitting in it. The old lady was very angry and <u>said to the men that they were sitting in her car</u>. She said that she wanted them to get out. When the men refused, she took a gun out of her bag, and the terrified men ran away.

Then she and her friend got into the car but she couldn't start the car. She said that it was the wrong key and that it didn't fit. Then she noticed an identical car nearby. She said to her friend that this wasn't her car. They went to the police station and said to the police officer that they had accidentally stolen a car. The police officer laughed and pointed to four frightened men. He said that they had arrived at the police station a few minutes ago and had reported the theft of the car by two dangerous old ladies.

The old lady said to the men, 'You're ...

8 **SPEAKING** Act out the story in groups. Use direct speech.

Computer crime

I can understand and react to an article about a crime.

1 Quickly read the first two paragraphs of the text. What was Sven Jaschan's crime?

1 He stole computers.
2 He created a computer virus.
3 He used his computer to steal millions of dollars.

Exam tip

In multiple choice tasks, underline the key words in the questions. Then look for the same words in the text. This way you will find it easier to identify the information you need.

2 Read the text. Choose the best answers.

1 How far did the virus spread?
  a All around Germany.
  b All around the world.
  c To Japan, Hong Kong, Australia and the USA.

2 Why wasn't Sven sent to prison?
  a Because he was too young.
  b Because he wasn't found guilty.
  c Because he admitted his guilt to detectives.

3 How did he feel after he'd released the virus?
  a At first he was frightened, then he was delighted.
  b He was delighted that he'd caused a lot of damage, but terrified that he might be caught.
  c At first he was delighted, then he became frightened.

4 How did the police catch him?
  a One of his classmates told Microsoft about him.
  b Detectives came to his home to ask questions.
  c The police offered a $250,000 reward.

5 How did Sven's teachers react?
  a They thought one of Sven's classmates had created the virus.
  b They were surprised because Sven wasn't the best student in information technology lessons.
  c They thought that Sven was clever enough to create the virus.

3 Match the 'extreme' adjectives highlighted in the text with the definitions below.

1 very important   4 very surprised   7 very bad
2 very big   5 very clever   8 very good
3 very small   6 very happy   9 very scared

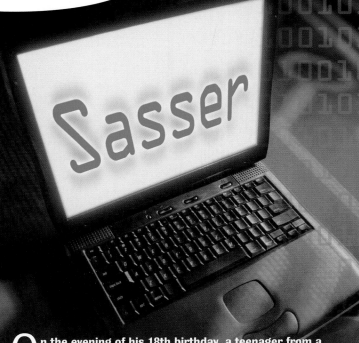

On the evening of his 18th birthday, a teenager from a tiny village in northern Germany clicked 'send' on his computer. Within three hours, the postal service in Taiwan was in chaos, computers in hospitals and banks in Hong Kong
5 had crashed, and trains in Australia and the USA had stopped.

In court a few months later, the teenager, Sven Jaschan, was charged with criminal damage. He was found guilty of putting the terrible 'Sasser' computer virus on the Internet and received a 21-month suspended sentence. He avoided
10 prison because he was only eighteen when he committed the crime. The virus infected millions of computer systems across the world, and caused millions of dollars of damage.

Sven admitted his guilt to the detectives who came to his home last year. He had spent an **enormous** amount of time
15 creating the Sasser virus on the computer in his bedroom. He often spent ten hours a day in front of his computer but his parents hadn't known what he was doing at the time.

When he released the virus on the Internet, he didn't realise it would cause so much damage. He was just **delighted** that
20 it had worked. 'I felt as if I had written a first-class essay', said Sven. 'I told my classmates — they thought it was **terrific**.' But his feelings changed very quickly. He was **terrified** when he saw a TV news report about the virus and the damage it had caused.

25 Detectives arrested Sven after one of his classmates contacted Microsoft and told them about him. Microsoft had offered a $250,000 reward for information about the virus. However, Sven's teachers at school were **astonished** that Sven had created the virus. They said that he wasn't a
30 **brilliant** computer student. 'There are others in the class who are better than him,' one teacher said!

While he was waiting for his trial to start, Sven left school and started work. He now works for a computer company, making 'firewalls' — **vital** pieces of software that protect
35 computers from viruses!

4 🎧 2.33 **PRONUNCIATION** Listen and repeat. Pay attention to the intonation.

> Were you surprised?

> Surprised? I was astonished!

5 🎧 2.34 **PRONUNCIATION** Work in pairs. Reply to the sentences using extreme adjectives. Then listen, repeat and check.

1 Is Jane's computer very small?

> Small? It's tiny.

2 Were you happy with your exam results?
3 Is this information important?
4 Is she clever?
5 Are you scared of spiders?
6 Was the film bad?
7 Is their house big?

6 Imagine that a virus caused every computer system in your country to crash. What would happen?

7 **SPEAKING** Work in pairs. Answer the questions.

1 Why do you think people create computer viruses?
  a they are vandals
  b they want people to notice and admire them
  c it is a challenge – they want to see if it's possible
  d they are bored and have nothing better to do
  e another reason

  > I think people create computer viruses because …

2 Why do you think Sven created the Sasser virus?
3 In your opinion, should people who create computer viruses go to prison? Why?/Why not?

  > I think they should … because …

  > I don't think they should … because …

Reporting a theft

I can report a theft and describe what was stolen.

Police officer	Good afternoon. How can I help?
Sarah	I think someone has stolen my bag.
Officer	OK, I'll just take some details. Could you tell me where and when you last had it?
Sarah	I think I left it in a café in King Street, about an hour ago.
Officer	And you've been back to the café to see if it's there?
Sarah	Yes, I went straight back but it wasn't there.
Officer	Can you describe it?
Sarah	Yes, it's blue and white. It's made of canvas.
Officer	Can you tell me what was in the bag?
Sarah	Yes, my wallet, some make-up, a pen and some keys.
Officer	OK. Was there any identification in the bag?
Sarah	I'm not sure.
Officer	That's fine. Could you fill in this form, please?

1 🎧 2.35 **Read and listen to the dialogue. What was stolen? When and where did it happen?**

2 SPEAKING **Work in pairs. Practise reading the dialogue, changing the words in blue. Use the information from the box.**

Item stolen	Where and when?	Colour	Material	Contents
wallet	shop, at about 11 o'clock	black	leather	£20 in cash
schoolbag	Internet café, two hours ago	green	canvas	schoolbooks, pens
sports bag	park, just now	white	plastic	trainers, tracksuit

3 🎧 2.36 **Listen to the dialogues. Which of Lenka's items were stolen? Which of Malcolm's items were stolen?**

bus pass	bag	credit card	wallet	mobile phone
schoolbag	traveller's cheques	£10	postcards	

4 🎧 2.36 **Listen again. Choose the correct answers.**

1 When did Lenka realise that her wallet was missing?
   a an hour ago
   b 30 minutes ago
   c 15 minutes ago

2 What advice does the police officer give to Lenka?
   a She should go back to the shop.
   b She should contact the credit card company.
   c She should contact the travel insurance company.

3 What colour is Lenka's wallet, and what is it made of?
   a blue, made of leather
   b black, made of plastic
   c black, made of leather

4 What had the thief done with Malcolm's schoolbag?
   a He had thrown it into a garden.
   b He had thrown it into a river.
   c He had given it to someone.

5 What make and model was the mobile?
   a Nokia 6260
   b Nokia 6060
   c Nokia 6062

6 What does the officer ask Malcolm to do?
   a get a new bus pass
   b get a new mobile
   c fill in a form

5 SPEAKING **Work in pairs. Prepare a dialogue in a police station following the chart below.**

Police officer

Greet the person. Ask if you can help.

Student

→ Tell the officer that someone has stolen your bag.

Ask when and where it happened. ←

→ Answer the question.

Ask for a description of the bag. ←

→ Answer the question.

Ask what was in the bag. ←

→ Answer the question.

Ask for a description of the item(s) in the bag. ←

→ Answer the question.

Give some advice. What should he/she do now? ←

→ Thank the officer.

6 SPEAKING **Act out your dialogue to the class.**

WRITING

A story

I can write a story describing a crime.

1 **Read the story quickly. Why did Jeremy want to buy a sat nav system (satellite navigation system)?**

> The careless thief
>
> One evening last week, Jeremy Watkins was trying to buy a second-hand sat nav system for his car from an online auction site.
>
> Two weeks earlier, a thief had stolen the sat nav system from Jeremy's car. Unfortunately, since the car wasn't locked, the insurance company had refused to replace the system.
>
> After a while Jeremy found some sat nav systems for sale. As he was looking at them, he was astonished to see his own system for sale. Jeremy immediately bought it and e-mailed the seller to say that he would come round to his house the following day to collect it. Then he phoned the police.
>
> The next day, a police officer called at the man's house. He pretended to be Jeremy. As soon as the man gave him the sat nav system, the police officer arrested him. So in the end Jeremy got his system back!

2 **Put the events in the correct order.**

- ☐ Jeremy got his old sat nav system back.
- ☐ A police officer went to the thief's house and arrested him.
- ☐ A thief stole Jeremy's sat nav system.
- ☐ Jeremy rang the police.
- ☐ Jeremy saw his own sat nav system for sale and bought it.
- ☐ Jeremy left his car unlocked.
- ☐ The insurance company refused to pay for a new sat nav system.
- ☐ Jeremy found an auction site that had sat nav systems for sale.
- ☐ Jeremy sent an e-mail to the thief.

3 **Find ten of these time expressions in the story and underline them. Translate all of them.**

> **Time expressions**
> in the end   after a while   at first   immediately   soon
> then   one (evening)   last (week)   (two weeks) earlier
> the following (day)   the next (day)   as soon as   as   while

4 **Choose the correct time expressions.**

1 There's a fire – please leave the building **in the end / immediately**.
2 The police arrested her because **a week earlier / the following week** she'd stolen a mobile phone.
3 Somebody attacked him **as / as soon as** he was walking through the park.
4 **At first / After a while** I thought he was innocent, but **immediately / in the end** I realised he was lying.
5 The witness identified the criminal **as soon as / while** she saw him.

Writing tip

Use time expressions to order the events in a story.

5 **Cover the story and exercise 2. Use the pictures to retell the story.**

6 **Do this writing task. First make notes, using the ideas below to help you.**

> **Write a crime story. Write 130–150 words.**

- What was the crime?
- Who were the criminals?
- What did they do?
- Who was the victim?
- Were there any witnesses?
- Did the police catch the criminals? If so, how?

Check your work

Have you

- ☐ used some time expressions to order the events?
- ☐ thought of a good title for your story?
- ☐ written 130–150 words?
- ☐ checked your spelling, punctuation and grammar?

1 **Get ready to LISTEN** Match four of the words in the box with the photos.

Natural disasters earthquake flood forest fire hurricane tornado storm tsunami volcanic eruption

2 2.37 Do the Listening exam task.

LISTENING exam task

Listen to the radio documentary about hurricanes.
Are the sentences true (T) or false (F)?

	True	False
1 The wind speed in hurricanes is greater than 115 km/h.	☐	☐
2 1,600 people have been killed by hurricanes since 2005.	☐	☐
3 Hurricane's don't travel very fast over the sea.	☐	☐
4 Professor Keane explains why hurricanes can cause floods.	☐	☐
5 In the programme you could hear details about the British weather.	☐	☐

3 SPEAKING What kind of natural disasters or extreme weather occur in your country? What problems do they cause?

4 **Get ready to SPEAK** Match the geographical features 1–6 in the picture with the words from the box. Which geographical feature isn't illustrated?

Geographical features cave forest island lake mountains river sand dunes

5 **Get ready to SPEAK** Match the words with the photos. Some words can go with both photos.

boat crops drought drown dry flood food grow rain rise starve water

6 Match 1–5 with a–e. Who would say these things: people in a flood, people in a drought, or both?

1 We can't grow any crops,
2 If the water rises higher,
3 We were rescued from our house
4 It hasn't rained
5 The water has flooded our house

a by some people in a boat.
b and ruined everything.
c so we haven't got any food.
d for six months.
e there's a danger that the animals in the fields will drown.

7 Do the Speaking exam task.

SPEAKING exam task

Compare and contrast the two photos of the flood and the drought. Think about these things:

1 What problems do floods cause?
2 What problems do droughts cause?
3 How can we help people in these situations?

1 Get ready to READ Quickly read the text about the island of Alcatraz. Which sentence is true?

1 The prisoners weren't allowed visitors.
2 Lots of people successfully escaped from Alcatraz.
3 Alcatraz isn't a prison now.

2 Do the Reading exam task.

READING exam task

Seven sentences have been removed from the text. Choose from sentences a–h the one that best fits each gap. There is one extra sentence that you don't need.

a The three men disappeared one night and were never seen again.
b Most men could extend their arms and touch the wall on either side.
c Thirty-six men tried to escape, including two who tried to escape twice.
d It is hard to get to and it is even harder to escape from.
e However, the prison was finally closed in 1963.
f The other five are still listed as 'missing'.
g Most people think they drowned trying to swim over to the shore.
h So they started building a prison, and from the 1930s to the 1960s, Alcatraz was America's top security prison.

Alcatraz

Every year over one million tourists board the ferry from San Francisco and visit Alcatraz, which was once the toughest prison in the USA.

Alcatraz is a small, rocky island in the San Francisco Bay. **1** ☐ It is isolated and surrounded by icy cold waters with dangerous currents. It was first a military fortress, but by the end of the 1860s the army realised it was an ideal place for putting dangerous prisoners. **2** ☐

The cells were very small. Each cell measured just 1.5 metres by 2.7 metres. **3** ☐ Each cell had a small sink and toilet, and a narrow bed. Prisoners weren't allowed to talk to each other much, and there were very strict rules with harsh punishments for those who broke them. Each prisoner was allowed one visitor per month.

In spite of the difficulty of getting from the island to the mainland, there were many attempts by prisoners to escape. **4** ☐ Twenty-three men were recaptured, six others were shot and killed during their escape, and two drowned trying

3 Get ready to SPEAK Match the words with the photos. Which other words might you need to describe them?

> cell   clothes   food   free   happy   lonely   prison   prisoner   punish   visitor

4 Do the Speaking exam task.

SPEAKING exam task

Choose one of the photos and speak about it. Talk about:
- who the people are
- where they are
- what's happening in the photo.

Now compare the photos. These ideas may help you.

1 How are life in prison and normal life different?
2 How are the people in the photos feeling?

to swim across the bay. **5** ☐ The Hollywood film *Escape from Alcatraz* tells the story of three of those men. Clint Eastwood played the part of real-life prisoner Frank Morris, who, along with two friends planned a very clever escape over seven months. **6** ☐ The police looked for them for years but nobody knows what happened to them.

7 ☐ After all, if someone had managed to escape from Alcatraz, they would want to reappear and tell the world about it somehow!

10 The written word

THIS UNIT INCLUDES ●●●●●
Vocabulary • publications • books and text • styles of fiction
• bookshop departments • talking about stories
Grammar • the passive (present simple) • the passive (other tenses)
Speaking • talking about reading habits • in a bookshop
Writing • a book review

A VOCABULARY AND LISTENING
Publications

I can identify and talk about different publications.

1 Can you match the titles of the books 1–8 with the writers in the box?

> Jane Austen   Agatha Christie
> Joseph Conrad   Charles Dickens
> Stephen King   J. K. Rowling
> J. R. R. Tolkien   William Shakespeare

1 Hamlet
2 Murder on the Orient Express
3 The Lord of the Rings
4 Oliver Twist
5 Harry Potter and the Philosopher's Stone
6 The Shining
7 Pride and Prejudice
8 Lord Jim

2 Have you read any of the books in exercise 1?
Do you know any other books by the same authors?

3 🎧 2.38 **PRONUNCIATION** Listen and repeat the list of publications in the box. Underline the stress in each word.

> **Publications** atlas autobiography biography comic
> cookbook dictionary encyclopaedia guidebook
> magazine manual newspaper novel play textbook

4 Which publication from exercise 3 would you read if you wanted to:

1 find out which country Timbuktu was in?
2 look up a word you didn't understand?
3 learn about spiders?
4 learn how your new DVD recorder works?
5 read the latest gossip about Hollywood stars?
6 read stories with lots of pictures and not many words?
7 prepare for a maths exam?
8 find out what to do and see when you're on holiday?
9 find out how to cook a nice meal?
10 read about what is happening in the world?
11 read about the life of a famous person, written by that person?
12 read about the life of a famous person, written by another person?
13 read a long story?
14 read something written for the theatre?

> ●●●●● Vocabulary Builder (part 1): page 133

5 🎧 2.39 Listen to two teenagers, Josh and India, doing a questionnaire. Complete the questions.

1 _____ favourite authors?
2 How much _____ ?
3 When _____ ?
4 Would _____ write?
5 What _____ about?

6 🎧 2.39 Listen again. Choose the answers that India and Josh give. Write *a* or *b* in the table below.

1 **a** Stephen King and Agatha Christie
  b Jane Austen and Charles Dickens
2 **a** about an hour a day   **b** about two hours a day
3 **a** before and after school **b** in the evening
4 **a** yes   **b** no
5 **a** crime and violence   **b** love and romance

	1	2	3	4	5
India					
Josh					

7 **SPEAKING** Work in pairs. Do the questionnaire answering questions from exercise 5. Tell the class about your partner.

> ●●●●● Vocabulary Builder (part 2): page 133

1 Read the text. What do the numbers refer to?

1 1851   2 40   3 1.3 million

The New York Times is one the most famous papers in the world. It first appeared in 1851. Today, it is known for the accuracy and quality of its journalism. It is owned by the New York Times Company, which also publishes 40 other newspapers. Over 1.3 million copies are printed every day, and it is published online too.

2 Look at the example of the passive in blue in the text. Then read and complete the rule in the *Learn this!* box.

> **LEARN THIS!**
>
> **1** The **present passive** is formed with the correct form of the verb _____ and the past participle.
>
> *This TV show is filmed in Spain.*
> *Magazines aren't sold in that shop.*
> *Is this newspaper printed in China?*
>
> **2** When we want to say who performed the action, we use *by*.
> *This book is published by Oxford University Press.*

3 Find three more examples of the passive in the text in exercise 1. Are they singular or plural? Do they say who performed the action?

4 Choose the correct words to complete the sentences about *The Big Issue* magazine.

1 *The Big Issue* **is** / **are** published every week.
2 Some of the articles **is** / **are** written by famous people.
3 About 160,000 copies of each issue **is** / **are** sold in the UK.
4 The magazine **is** / **are** sold by homeless people for £1.40 a copy.
5 The people who sell the magazine **is** / **are** known as 'vendors'.
6 About half of the money from sales **is** / **are** kept by the vendors.
7 The other half **is** / **are** used by the vendors to buy more magazines.
8 Special badges **is** / **are** worn by the vendors.

• • • • • Grammar Builder (10B): page 122

5 🎧 2.40 Listen and number the pictures in the correct order. Complete the sentences with the present simple passive.

How paper is made

☐ The mixture _____ (press) onto large flat metal sheets.

☐ The rolls of paper _____ (send) to factories where they _____ (make) into books, magazines and hundreds of other things.

☐ The sheets of paper _____ (dry). Then they _____ (put) onto big rolls.

☐ Trees _____ (grow) on a 'tree farm'. The trees _____ (cut down), then new trees _____ (plant).

☐ The chips _____ (cook) with a lot of water.

☐ The wood _____ (take) by lorry to the paper mill where it _____ (cut) into very small pieces called 'chips'.

6 **SPEAKING** Work in pairs. Think of as many examples as you can of these things. Which pair has the most ideas?

1 newspapers that are published every day
2 things that are made in your country
3 sports that aren't played in your country
4 things that are eaten at Christmas
5 fruits that aren't grown in your country

1 Can you name any plays by William Shakespeare? Have you seen any on TV, or in the cinema or theatre?

2 Read the text. What do the dates and numbers refer to?

1	1564	4	1585
2	15	5	1597
3	26	6	37

3 Are the sentences true or false?

1 Shakespeare was born in the sixteenth century.
2 He originally worked in business.
3 He got married and had four children.
4 We don't know why he left Stratford and became an actor.
5 He became quite rich from writing plays.
6 He stopped writing and acting five years before he died.
7 He stayed in London until his death.
8 He was born and died on the same date.

4 🎧 2.41 Listen to the interviews. Match speakers 1–3 with the plays that they are studying.

 ①  ②  ③

Andy   Sarah   Mike

a *Julius Caesar*
b *Romeo and Juliet*
c *Hamlet*

5 🎧 2.41 Listen again. Whose opinions are these? Write A (Andy), S (Sarah) or M (Mike).

1 The stories are fantastic.
2 Shakespeare is too difficult.
3 Shakespeare's plays should be seen at the theatre.
4 Shakespeare is old-fashioned.
5 The characters in the plays are interesting.
6 Shakespeare writes about important things.

6 Complete the sentences with the words in the box.

Types of literature	plays	poems	novels	short stories

1 A playwright writes _____ .
2 A novelist writes _____ and/or _____ .
3 A poet writes _____ .

7 **SPEAKING** Name some famous writers from your country. Can you remember any of their works?

> Ernest Hemingway was a novelist. One of his most famous works is the novel *For Whom the Bell Tolls*.

William Shakespeare

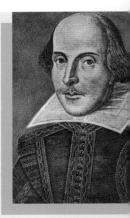

William Shakespeare is probably the most famous playwright in history. He was born on 23 April 1564 in Stratford-upon-Avon in England. He was one of eight brothers and sisters. His father, John Shakespeare, was a successful businessman. William went to school in Stratford and learned Latin and Greek, but he didn't go to university. At the age of fifteen he went to work in his father's business.

When he was eighteen, he met and fell in love with Anne Hathaway. She was eight years older than him. They got married in November 1582, and six months later their daughter Susanna was born. In 1585 they had twins, Hamnet and Judith. Little is known about the next seven years of his life. We only know that he moved to London, leaving Anne and the children in Stratford, and that by 1592 he was writing plays and working as an actor.

His plays were very popular and he made a lot of money. In 1597 he bought a big house in Stratford for his family, but he stayed in London for another thirteen years. He continued to write and act and also bought a theatre. In 1611 he finally retired and moved back to Stratford to live in the house he had bought. In total, Shakespeare wrote 37 plays and 154 sonnets (fourteen-line poems). Some of his love poems are addressed to a married woman, and some of them are addressed to a young man. Nobody knows the identity of these two people.

Shakespeare died in Stratford on his birthday, on 23 April 1616, and was buried in the church where he had been christened exactly 52 years earlier.

I can use different forms of the passive.

1 What is the book in the photo? Read the text and find out.

𝒯he Bible is the world's most popular book. Over 100 million copies are sold every year. The Bible probably wasn't written until about 50 years after Jesus's death. It was written in Hebrew and Greek, but it has been translated into over two thousand languages. How many bibles have been printed? No one knows exactly, but it's probably more than six billion.

2 Underline the passive forms in the text and match them with the tenses. Complete the table.

The passive	
1 present simple affirmative	Over 100 million copies are sold every year.
2 past simple affirmative	
3 past simple negative	
4 present perfect affirmative	
5 present perfect interrogative	

⬤⬤⬤⬤ **Grammar Builder (10D): page 122**

3 Match the active and passive sentences with the same meaning and complete them.

Active
1 Tolkien _____ *The Lord of the Rings* in the 1950s.
2 They have translated a Harry Potter book into Latin!
3 They first _____ *Hamlet* in London in 1601.
4 People know J.K. Rowling for the Harry Potter stories.
5 Spielberg _____ his film *Jaws* on a book by Peter Benchley.
6 Ian Fleming created the character James Bond.

Passive
a *Hamlet* was first performed in London in 1601.
b The character James Bond _____ by Ian Fleming.
c The film *Jaws* is based on a book by Peter Benchley.
d A Harry Potter book _____ into Latin!
e *The Lord of the Rings* was written by Tolkien in the 1950s.
f J.K. Rowling _____ for the Harry Potter stories.

4 Complete the text with the passive form of the verbs in brackets.

Wiki Websites

'Wiki' means 'quick' in Hawaiian. The word ¹_____ (use) to describe websites that ²_____ (write) by the people who use the site. Anyone who visits a wiki website can add or change the information on the page. The first wiki website ³_____ (create) by Ward Cunningham in 1995. Since then, wiki guidebooks, wiki dictionaries and wiki encyclopaedias ⁴_____ (publish) on the Internet. The most popular online encyclopaedia is 'Wikipedia'. Over 22 million entries ⁵_____ (add) since it started, and it is now the most detailed encyclopaedia in the world. According to the creator of Wikipedia, the work ⁶_____ (do) by 20,000 people who regularly edit the pages. The amazing thing is that the information is completely free.

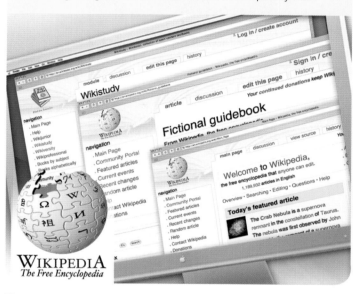

5 Complete the questions with the correct passive form (present simple, past simple or present perfect) of the verbs in brackets.

1 What item of clothing _____ (ban) from some shopping centres and schools in England?
2 Where _____ the Oxford and Cambridge boat race _____ (hold) every year?
3 Who _____ (attack) by a shark in Hawaii in 2003?
4 Which two languages _____ (speak) today in Wales?
5 Which actors _____ (choose) to play James Bond in the Bond films?
6 Name one film that _____ (direct) by Milos Forman.
7 What kind of food _____ (sell) at a butcher's shop?
8 When _____ the Palace of Culture in Warsaw _____ (complete)?

6 **SPEAKING** Work in pairs. Ask and answer the questions in exercise 5. The answers are all in units 1–5 of this book.

A teenage writer

*I can understand an
interview with an author.*

1 Check the meaning of the words in the box in your dictionary. Then choose your favourite and least favourite style of fiction. Give reasons.

> **Styles of fiction** classic novels   comic novels   crime   fantasy   historical novels   horror   romantic fiction   science fiction   short stories

2 Quickly read the text. Which two styles of fiction are mentioned?

> **Exam tip**
>
> When you look for specific information in a text, read the questions carefully. They will help you identify the information in the text.

3 Choose the best definitions for the highlighted words in the text.

1 educated
  a banned, prohibited   **b** taught
2 a best-seller
  a a very popular book   **b** a very good book
3 intended
  a planned to do something   **b** failed to do something
4 as long as
  a because   **b** if
5 telepathy
  a TV programmes   **b** the ability to know what is in somebody's mind
6 persistent
  a lazy   **b** not stopping or giving up
7 disciplined
  a well-organised   **b** angry
8 humble
  a not thinking you are too important **b** funny
9 criticism
  a other people's opinions   **b** money

4 Complete the questions with the words in the box.

> How   What   When   Where   Which   Who   Why

1 _____ did Christopher Paolini have lessons?
2 _____ did he begin writing his first novel?
3 _____ is the name of his first novel?
4 _____ published his first novel?
5 _____ did Paolini continue to write novels?
6 _____ can teach you more about people's feelings: books or TV?
7 _____ can young people improve their writing?

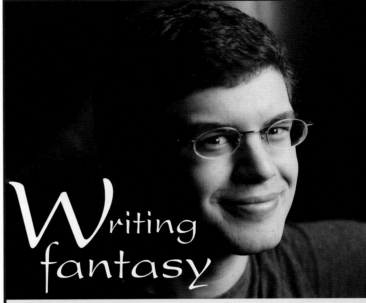

Writing fantasy

Christopher Paolini had an unusual childhood. He didn't go to school. He was educated at home by his parents. He began writing his first novel, *Eragon*, when he was fifteen. It is about a magical land called Alagaësia. The novel was published privately by his parents in 2002 and it quickly became a best-seller. In this interview, Christopher talks about his work.

Interviewer When did you decide to become a writer?

Christopher I've known for a long time that I wanted to tell stories, with books, movies, or plays. In fact, *Eragon* was originally an idea for a movie. I never really intended to become an author. Of course, since it worked out so well, I've continued to write.

Interviewer Who are your favourite authors?

Christopher Philip Pullman, Mervyn Peake, J.R.R. Tolkien, E.R. Eddison, Garth Nix, Octavia Butler, and many, many more. I also love science fiction. *Dune*, by Frank Herbert is a favourite. Anything – as long as it's good!

Interviewer What do you like about science fiction and fantasy stories?

Christopher I enjoy fantasy because I can visit lands that have never existed, see things that never could exist, experience adventures with interesting characters, and, most importantly, feel the sense of magic in the world.

Interviewer Do you get a lot of letters from your fans?

Christopher Yes, I do. My favourite one came from a woman who enjoyed *Eragon* so much that she named her pet spider 'Saphira', after the dragon in my book!

Interviewer Why should teenagers read when they have TV, computer games, the Internet …?

Christopher Books can take you deeper into people's thoughts and feelings than TV or radio. Until we invent telepathy , books are our best choice for understanding the rest of humanity.

Interviewer What advice would you give to young people who'd like to write?

Christopher Three simple things: Write about what excites you the most. Be persistent and disciplined. Be humble enough to accept criticism and learn all you can about writing.

5 SPEAKING Work in pairs. Ask and answer the questions in exercise 4.

6 🎧 2.42 Read and listen to the song. Which sentence is correct?

1 A writer is addressing a publisher.
2 A publisher is addressing a writer.

Paperback writer
by the Beatles

Paperback writer (writer, writer)
Dear Sir or Madam, will you read my book?
It took me years to write – will you take a look?
It's based on a novel by a man named Lear,
And I need a job, so I want to be a paperback writer,
Paperback writer.

It's the dirty story of a dirty man
And his clinging wife doesn't understand.
His son is working for the Daily Mail,
It's a steady job but he wants to be a paperback writer,
Paperback writer.

Paperback writer (writer, writer)

It's a thousand pages, give or take a few,
I'll be writing more in a week or two.
I can make it longer if you like the style,
I can change it round and I want to be a paperback writer,
Paperback writer.

If you really like it you can have the rights,
It could make a million for you overnight.
If you must return it, you can send it here,
But I need a break and I want to be a paperback writer,
Paperback writer.

Paperback writer (writer, writer)

7 Underline the parts of the song where the writer says:

1 how long the book is
2 that he can write more, or change the story if they want him to
3 what the book is about
4 that it will make a lot of money
5 why he wants to be a writer
6 where the publisher should send it if he/she doesn't like it
7 how long he has spent writing the book

8 Match the colloquial expressions from the song 1–3 with the meanings a–c. Then find the expressions in the song.

1 I need a break   a in a very short time
2 overnight   b approximately
3 give or take [a few]   c I need some luck

9 SPEAKING Work in pairs. Student A: You are the writer from the song. Tell the publisher why he/she should publish your book. Use your own ideas and the information from the song but do not quote any of the lyrics in your response.
Student B: You are the publisher from the song. Ask the writer questions and decide if you want to publish his/her book. You must not quote any of the song's lyrics in your response.

Buying books

I can ask for information in a bookshop.

Darren	Good morning. I wonder if you could help me. I'm looking for a book called *Computing Made Easy*.
Shop assistant	It'll be over there in the Science and Technology section.
Darren	I've looked but I can't see it on the shelves.
Assistant	Let me just check on the computer ... Do you know the name of the author?
Darren	I think it's Hammond.
Assistant	Ah, yes. No, I'm sorry, we don't have it in stock. But I can order it for you.
Darren	Yes, please. How much is it?
Assistant	£12.99.
Darren	And how long will it take?
Assistant	About a week or ten days.
Darren	That's fine.
Assistant	OK, if I could just take some details ...

1 🎧 2.43 **Read and listen to the dialogue. Answer the questions.**

1 Why doesn't Darren get the book that he wants?
2 When will he get it?

2 SPEAKING **Work in pairs. Practise reading the dialogue, changing the words in blue. Use words from the box and your own ideas.**

> **Bookshop departments** adult fiction   art   biography
> children's fiction   cookery   health and fitness   history
> humour   languages   nature   poetry and drama
> reference   science and technology   sport   travel

3 🎧 2.44 **Listen to three customers in a bookshop. Which customer leaves the shop with a book?**

4 **Complete the sentences from the dialogues using the prepositions in the box.**

> by   by   down   for   on   on   out   under   up

1 I'm looking _____ a book _____ Stephen King.
2 I'm afraid we've sold _____ of that book.
3 It's already _____ order.
4 Try looking _____ 'languages'.
5 Can I pay _____ credit card?
6 I'll look it _____ on the computer.
7 It will be here _____ Friday.
8 Can you write _____ your name and telephone number?

5 🎧 2.45 **Listen and check.**

6 SPEAKING **Work in pairs. Prepare a dialogue in a bookshop following the chart below.**

Shop assistant

Greet the customer.
Ask if you can help.

Customer

Say what book you need.

Tell the customer where to look for it.

Say that you can't find it.

Suggest ordering it.

Ask how long it will take.

Reply.

Decide to order it/not to order it.

Exam tip

Go to the *Functions Bank* in the Workbook for more phrases and expressions you can use in a conversation.

---

7 SPEAKING **Act out your dialogue to the class.**

WRITING
A book review

I can write a review of a book.

1 Read the book review. In which paragraph does Joanna:

1 give her opinion of the book?
2 describe what happens in the book?
3 give brief information about the book and its author?

A book review

by Joanna

One of my favourite books is *Northern Lights* by Philip Pullman. It's a fantasy story set in Oxford and it's the first part of a trilogy.

It's the story of a girl called Lyra. She tries to save some children who have been kidnapped by a strange woman called Mrs Coulter. Lyra and some friends travel north to look for the missing children, who include her best friend, Roger. The ending is very exciting, with an interesting twist, but I won't give it away.

I liked the book for a number of reasons. The author has created an amazing fantasy world. The story is very gripping and I found it difficult to put down. The characters are convincing, and I identified strongly with Lyra. The book is sometimes compared with the Harry Potter stories. But I think it's more thought-provoking and less childish. I thoroughly recommend it.

2 Are the sentences true or false?

1 *Northern Lights* was written by Philip Pullman.
2 The story is set in London.
3 The main character is a girl.
4 Joanna didn't like the book.
5 Joanna thinks it's better than Harry Potter.

3 How many phrases from the box can you find in the review?

Talking about stories	
I identified with (*a character*)	It's the story of …
I liked the book because …	It was made into a film.
In the end, …	The main character is (*name*)
It was written by (*author*)	There's a twist at the end.
It's a (*type of story*)	I thoroughly recommend it
It's set in (*place*)	The ending is (*very exciting*).

4 Complete the text about *The Lord of the Rings*. Use phrases from the box in exercise 3.

The Lord of the Rings is a fantasy story. ¹_____ J. R. R. Tolkien. ²_____ an imaginary land called 'Middle Earth', and ³_____ a group of hobbits who have to destroy a magic ring. ⁴_____ called Frodo. ⁵_____ they succeed in destroying the ring. A few years ago ⁶_____ . Did you see it at the cinema? Anyway, it's a great book – ⁷_____ !

5 Choose a book that you have read. Write notes under these headings, but include any other information that you think is important.

- **Paragraph 1: General information**
  Title, author and type of book.

- **Paragraph 2: Story and characters**
  Where is it set? Who are the main characters? What happens?

- **Paragraph 3: Your opinion**
  Why did you like it? For example:
  It's funny/moving/exciting/gripping/interesting.
  It contains lots of interesting characters.
  I really wanted to know what was going to happen.
  There are lots of surprises.

6 Read the writing tip and do this writing task. Use your notes from exercise 5.

Writing tip

Remember to use the *present simple* to summarise the plot of a story or a film.

Write a review of a book you enjoyed. Write 130–150 words.

Check your work

Have you

☐ divided your review into three paragraphs?
☐ used some phrases from exercise 3?
☐ written 130–150 words?
☐ checked your spelling, punctuation and grammar?

Vocabulary

1 Complete the chart with the missing verbs and nouns.

Verb	Criminal
burgle a house	1 _____
2 _____ somebody	murderer
vandalise something	3 _____
4 _____ a bank	robber
sell drugs	5 _____
6 _____ joyriding	joyrider

Mark [ ] /6

2 Now complete the words for the crimes in exercise 1.

1 burg _ _ _ _
2 mur _ _ _
3 vandal _ _ _
4 rob _ _ _ _
5 drug-d _ _ _ _ _ _
6 joyrid _ _ _

Mark [ ] /6

3 Complete the sentences with the publications in the box.

atlas   autobiography   cookbook   dictionary
guidebook   manual   play   textbook

1 She looked in the _____ for a map of Austria.
2 It's a great _____ with lots of good recipes for fish.
3 I read the _____ at home before we saw it at the theatre.
4 She tells stories about her childhood in her _____ .
5 If you don't know a word, look it up in a _____ .
6 I'm not sure how to copy photos from my digital camera to my computer – I'll look in the _____ .
7 We're using an interesting _____ in our history classes.
8 When we went to New York, we stayed at a hotel that we found in the _____ .

Mark [ ] /8

Grammar

4 Complete the sentences with the past perfect form of the verbs in the box.

not close   finish   go   leave   not revise   see

1 By the time I arrived at the cinema, the film _____ .
2 When I looked in my bag, I realised that I _____ my phone on the bus.
3 I phoned my friend at home, but she _____ out.
4 I did badly in the exam because I _____ .
5 She told the police what she _____ .
6 The burglars got in through the window because we _____ it.

Mark [ ] /6

5 Read the dialogue. Complete the reported speech by changing the tense of the verbs in the dialogue.

Sam There's a good action film on TV.
Julie I don't like action films.
Sam It's a great film. My friend saw it at the cinema.
Julie I prefer romantic comedies.
Sam We always watch romantic comedies.
Julie That isn't true. We watched a horror film last time!

Sam said that _there was_ a good action film on TV. Julie said that she [1] _____ action films. Sam said that it [2] _____ a great film, and that his friend [3] _____ it at the cinema. Julie said that she [4] _____ romantic comedies. Sam said that they always [5] _____ romantic comedies. Julie said that that [6] _____ true, and that they [7] _____ a horror film last time.

Mark [ ] /7

6 Rewrite the active sentences as passive sentences.

1 They print this newspaper in London.
   This newspaper is printed in London.
2 They wear these shoes in Holland.
3 They built this church five hundred years ago.
4 They've stolen my bike.
5 They don't eat pork in Iran.
6 They make pasta in Italy.
7 They didn't translate his first novel.
8 They've caught the robbers.

Mark [ ] /7

Everyday English

7 Number the lines of the dialogue in the correct order.

[ ] Can you tell me what was in it?
[ ] How can I help?
[ ] I think somebody has stolen my bag.
[ ] Yes. My wallet and my mobile phone.
[ ] No, there wasn't. Just some money.
[ ] Was there any identification in the wallet?

Mark [ ] /6

8 Complete the dialogue with questions a–d.

a How much is it?   c How long will it take?
b Do you know the name of the author?   d Have you got it in stock?

Customer I'm looking for a novel called *The Black Crystal*.
Assistant [1] _____
Customer I think it's Harris.
Assistant Let me check. Ah, yes, *The Black Crystal* by Tom Harris.
Customer [2] _____
Assistant No, we haven't. I'm sorry. But I can order it for you.
Customer [3] _____
Assistant It's £7.99.
Customer That's fine. [4] _____
Assistant Two or three days.

Mark [ ] /4

TOTAL [ ] /50

Speaking

1 Work in pairs. Ask and answer the questions.

1 What's the best book you have ever read? What was it about?
2 What's the last book you read? What was it about?
3 What different kinds of publications do you read or look at? How often?

Reading

2 Read the e-mail. Which paragraph talks about:

1 a crime?
2 a difficult decision?
3 a competition?

Dear Chloe

Hi! How are you? Everything is fine here.

A Did I tell you about Daniel, the next-door neighbour? Well, he had a barbecue yesterday and he invited me. There were about 30 people there, and it was really good fun. We played lots of games of badminton. In fact, I won the tournament – I beat Daniel in the final! (He pretended to be annoyed, but I don't think he was really.)

B Later, while we were all eating, drinking and chatting in the back garden, some wallets were stolen from the house. (Most of the guests had left their jackets inside.) We think somebody walked into the house from the street, took the wallets and ran away. Daniel called the police, but they said that they couldn't do anything.

C Daniel didn't tell me that it was his birthday, so I hadn't bought a present for him. It was really embarrassing! I want to buy him a present this afternoon and give it to him. He likes reading, but I don't know what kinds of books he likes. I know that he's interested in sport. What shall I get him? I can't decide. Help!

Write soon!
love
Joanna

3 Write the questions for these answers.

1 About 30.
2 Joanna won it.
3 Some wallets.
4 They said that they couldn't do anything.
5 Because Daniel didn't tell her that it was his birthday.

Writing

4 Imagine you are Joanna's friend, Chloe. Write a short reply to Joanna's e-mail. Give advice about what book to buy for Daniel's birthday. Use the plan to help you.

Paragraph 1
• Ask how Joanna is.
• React to the news of the theft.

Paragraph 2
• Suggest a book or type of book.
• Give reasons for your suggestion.

Paragraph 3
• Tell her you hope Daniel likes the book.
• Sign off.

Listening

5 🎧 2.46 Listen to the conversations. What does Joanna buy for Daniel?

6 🎧 2.46 Listen again. Answer the questions.

1 What building is next to the bookshop?
2 Why doesn't Joanna buy the biography of Michael Owen?
3 In what section of the bookshop does Joanna look for a book?
4 How much is the book that Joanna buys?
5 What does the shop assistant offer Joanna, and does she accept?
6 What does Daniel think of the present?

GRAMMAR BUILDER 1

1B Present simple and present continuous

1 Make the affirmative statements negative. Make the negative statements affirmative. → 1.1, 1.2

1 I wear a suit at school.
I don't wear a suit at school.

2 He doesn't like weddings.
3 She plays volleyball after school.
4 We live in London.
5 My uncle works in a factory.
6 I want a sandwich.

2 Complete the questions. → 1.2

1 What _____ at school?
She wears a tracksuit.
2 Where _____ swimming?
He goes swimming at the sports centre.
3 Why _____ computer games?
They play computer games because they enjoy them.
4 When _____ in the morning?
He gets up at 7.30.
5 How _____ to work?
He goes by bus.

3 Write sentences using the present continuous.
→ 1.4, 1.5

1 they / wear / tracksuits
They're wearing tracksuits.

2 she / chat / to her friend
3 I / not have / a shower
4 we / not win / the match
5 he / dance / really badly
6 you / not listen / to me

4 SPEAKING Work in pairs. Look at the picture. Ask and answer the questions using the present continuous.
→ 1.4, 1.5

1 he / wear / a hat?
Is he wearing a hat?
No, he isn't.

2 they / standing up?
3 he / smile?
4 they / eat / a pizza?
5 she / wear / jeans?
6 she / hold / a mobile phone?

5 Complete the pairs of sentences with the present simple or the present continuous form of the verbs in brackets. → 1.3, 1.6

1 a She always _____ (wear) a white top for work.
  b I _____ (wear) new shoes. Do you like them?
2 a We _____ (go) skiing next month.
  b They _____ (go) skiing every winter.
3 a I _____ (love) this music. What is it?
  b I _____ (enjoy) this music. What is it?
4 a Light _____ (travel) faster than sound.
  b That car _____ (travel) very fast. Be careful!
5 a My dad often _____ (sing) in the shower.
  b My brother _____ (sing). What a terrible noise!
6 a I _____ (not believe) him. It's a lie!
  b He _____ (not tell) the truth. It's a lie!

1D verb + infinitive or -ing form

6 Match the two halves of the sentences. → 1.7, 1.8

1 When he was four, he began …   a to pay for his lessons.
2 His mother agreed …   b practising every day.
3 He imagined …   c to study music at university.
4 He hoped …   d to learn the piano.
5 He didn't mind …   e becoming a famous pianist.

7 Complete the sentences with the infinitive or -ing form of the verbs in brackets. → 1.7, 1.8

1 He's pretending _____ (be) angry.
2 I can't help _____ (feel) nervous.
3 She doesn't enjoy _____ (wear) formal clothes.
4 Have you finished _____ (eat)?
5 I didn't expect _____ (pass) the exam.
6 Do you want _____ (watch) television?
7 I don't feel like _____ (go) home.
8 We decided _____ (have) lunch in a café.
9 Do you fancy _____ (play) tennis tomorrow?
10 I promise _____ (tell) you the truth.

Present simple

1.1

We form the present simple like this:

Affirmative	
I play	we play
you play	you play
he/she/it plays	they play

Spelling: 3rd person singular (he/she/it)
We add -s to the end of most verbs.
  + -s   start → starts   play → plays
We add -es if the verb ends in -ch, -ss, -sh or -o.
  + -es   teach → teaches   miss → misses
              do → does   go → goes
If the verb ends in a consonant + -y, we change -y to i and add -es.
  -y → -ies   study → studies   carry → carries

GRAMMAR REFERENCE ①

1.2

Negative	
Full form	**Short form**
I do not play	I don't play
you do not play	you don't play
he/she/it does not play	he/she/it doesn't play
you do not play	you don't play
we do not play	we don't play
they do not play	they don't play

Interrogative	Short answer
Do I play ...?	Yes, I do. / No, I don't.
Do you play ...?	Yes, you do. / No, you don't.
Does he/she/it play ...?	Yes, she does. / No, she doesn't.
Do we/you/they play ...?	Yes, we/you/they do. No, we/you/they don't.

1.3

We use the present simple:
- for something that always happens or happens regularly (e.g. every week, often, sometimes).
  Sally cycles to school every day.
- for facts.
  Cows eat grass.
- with certain verbs that are not used in continuous tenses, e.g. *believe, hate, like, love, need, know, prefer, want*.
  I like this music. (NOT I'm liking this music. ✗)

Present continuous

1.4

We form the present continuous like this:
- the correct form of *be* + the *-ing* form of the main verb.
  Daniel is eating.
  The class aren't listening.
  Are you playing?

1.5

Spelling: verb + *-ing* form
We add *-ing* to the end of most verbs.
  play + *-ing* → play**ing**
  study + *-ing* → study**ing**

If the verb ends in a consonant + *-e*, we usually drop the *-e* and add *-ing*.
  -e → -ing   write → writing
               make → making

If the verb ends in a short, accented vowel + a consonant, we double the consonant.
  -m → -mming   swim → swimming
  -g → gging   jog → jogging
  -p → pping   tap → tapping
  -t → tting   cut → cutting

1.6

We use the present continuous:
- for something that is happening now.
  Look! It's raining.
- for something that is happening temporarily, not necessarily at the moment of speaking.
  My mum's learning English in the evenings.
- for arrangements in the future.
  We're playing tennis tomorrow.

We don't use the present continuous:
- with certain verbs, e.g. *believe, hate, like, love, need, know, prefer, want*.
  I like this music. (NOT I'm liking this music. ✗)

Verb + infinitive or *-ing* form

1.7

When we put two verbs together, the second verb is usually in the infinitive or the *-ing* form.
I **want to go** home. (infinitive)
John **suggested playing** chess. (*-ing* form)
British teenagers **like to watch** TV. / British teenagers **like watching** TV. (infinitive or *-ing* form)

1.8

Below is a list of verbs that are followed by the infinitive, the *-ing* form, or both.

verb + infinitive		verb + *-ing* form		Verb + infinitive or *-ing* form
agree	offer	avoid	finish	begin
decide	prepare	can't help	imagine	continue
expect	pretend	can't stand	practise	hate
fail	promise	don't mind	spend time	like
hope	refuse	enjoy	suggest	love
manage	seem	fancy		prefer
mean	want	feel like		start

GRAMMAR BUILDER 2

2B Past simple

1 Write the past simple form of the regular verbs. → 2.1, 2.2

1 compete _____
2 finish _____
3 chat _____
4 cheer _____
5 miss _____
6 carry _____
7 hate _____
8 stop _____

2 Complete the sentences with the past simple affirmative form of the verbs in brackets. Some are regular and some are irregular. → 2.1, 2.2, 2.3

1 I _____ (know) all the answers to the quiz.
2 My sister _____ (win) the tournament.
3 Our team _____ (score) a goal in the first half.
4 I _____ (like) that film.
5 We _____ (leave) home in the morning.
6 You _____ (teach) me how to play chess.
7 They _____ (enjoy) watching the match last night.
8 I _____ (prefer) going to primary school.

3 Make the sentences in exercise 2 negative. → 2.4

4 Complete the dialogue with past simple questions and short answers. → 2.4

Jake   What ¹_____ (you / do) last night?
Sue   I went to the cinema.
Jake   What ²_____ (you / see)?
Sue   The new Matt Damon film.
Jake   ³_____ (you / enjoy) it?
Sue   Yes, ⁴_____. It was great.
Jake   ⁵_____ (your sister / go) with you?
Sue   No, ⁶_____.

5 Complete the text messages with *was*, *wasn't*, *were* and *weren't*. → 2.5

You ¹_____ at home this morning.
Where ²_____ you?

I ³_____ at the beach.

Really? But it ⁴_____ sunny. It ⁵_____ cold!

I know. It ⁶_____ my surfing lesson.

2D Past simple and past continuous

6 Complete the text with the past continuous form of the verbs in brackets. → 2.7, 2.8

At 9.30 p.m., we arrived at Mike's party. Mike ¹_____ (stand) in the kitchen. He ²_____ (eat) a pizza. We said hello, but he ³_____ (not listen). Sue and Callum ⁴_____ (dance) in the hall. Maria ⁵_____ (sit) on the stairs. She ⁶_____ (hold) her head in her hands. Her shoulders ⁷_____ (shake) but she ⁸_____ (not cry). She ⁹_____ (laugh)!

7 Complete the dialogue with the past continuous form of the verbs in brackets. → 2.7

Policeman   What ¹_____ (you / do) at 8 o'clock yesterday evening?
Man   I ²_____ (watch) TV?
Policeman   Really? What ³_____ (you / watch)?
Man   A film.
Policeman   What was it called?
Man   Er … I can't remember. I ⁴_____ (not pay) attention.
Policeman   I see. And why is your jacket wet?
Man   I ⁵_____ (wear) it this morning when I went out.
Policeman   But it ⁶_____ (not rain) this morning!

8 Complete the sentences with the past simple or past continuous form of the verbs in brackets. → 2.6, 2.8

1 The goalie _____ (catch) the ball and _____ (throw) it to the defender.
2 My dad _____ (get) home while I _____ (watch) an ice hockey match on TV.
3 The referee _____ (stop) the match because it _____ (snow).
4 The motorcyclist _____ (put on) his helmet and _____ (get on) the motorbike.
5 She _____ (break) her leg while she _____ (ski).
6 The Los Angeles Lakers _____ (score) 30 points in the last 10 minutes, but they _____ (not win) the game.
7 It _____ (not rain) so we _____ (play) volleyball in the park.
8 Maria _____ (surf) when she _____ (see) a shark near the beach.

GRAMMAR REFERENCE (2)

Past simple

2.1

The affirmative form of the past simple is the same for all persons, singular and plural (*I*, *you*, *he*, *we*, etc.).

I watched a football match last night.
She watched TV.
They watched a DVD.

2.2

Spelling: past simple (affirmative) form of regular verbs
We form the past simple (affirmative) form of regular verbs by adding *-ed* to the verb.

| + *-ed* | work → worked | play → played |

If the verb ends in *-e*, we add *-d*.

| + *-d* | dance → danced | smoke → smoked |

If the verb ends in a consonant + *-y*, we change *-y* to *i* and add *-ed*.

| *-y* → *-ied* | study → studied | cry → cried |

If the verb ends in a short accented vowel + a consonant, we double the consonant.

-p → *-pped*	drop → dropped
-n → *-nned*	plan → planned
-t → *-tted*	regret → regretted

2.3

Some verbs have irregular past simple (affirmative) forms. There are no spelling rules for these forms: you need to learn them by heart. See the list in the Workbook.

Irregular verbs behave in the same way as regular verbs in negative sentences and questions.

2.4

In negative sentences and questions we use *did/didn't* + the infinitive without *to* (NOT the past simple form) for regular and irregular verbs. The forms are the same for all persons, singular and plural (*I*, *you*, *he*, *we*, etc.).

Negative	Interrogative
I didn't watch.	Did I watch?
he/she/it didn't watch	Did he/she/it watch?
we/you/they didn't watch	Did we/you/they watch?

Short form and full form	Short answer
didn't = did not	Yes, I did. / No, I didn't.

2.5

The past simple forms of *be* are *was* or *were*.

Affirmative	Negative	Interrogative
I **was** sad	I **wasn't** sad	**Was** I sad?
you **were** sad	you **weren't** sad	**Were** you sad?
he/she/it **was** sad	he/she/it **wasn't** sad	**Was** he/she/ it sad?
we/you/they **were** sad	we/you/they **weren't** sad	**Were** we/you/they sad?

2.6

We use the past simple:
* for a completed action or event at a definite point in the past.
  We played volleyball last Saturday.
* for actions or events that happened one after another.
  Joanna got up, had a shower, got dressed and left the house.
* with certain verbs that are not used in continuous tenses, e.g. *believe, hate, like, love, need, know, prefer, want*.
  The police officer believed his story. (NOT ~~The police officer was believing his story.~~ ✗)

Past continuous

2.7

We form the past continuous like this:
* *was* or *were* + the *-ing* form of the main verb
  Elizabeth was eating.   The children weren't listening.
  Were you playing?

Spelling: verb + *-ing* form
See point 1.5.

We use the past continuous:
* to describe an action lasting for some time or serving as the background to other events.
  It was raining.   Some children were playing rugby.

We don't use the past continuous:
* with certain verbs, e.g. *believe, hate, like, love, need, know, prefer, want*.
  Tim needed a new car. (NOT ~~Tim was needing a new car.~~ ✗)

2.8

We often use the past continuous and the past simple in the same sentence. The past continuous describes a background action or event in the past; the past simple describes a shorter action or event that happened during the longer action, or interrupted it.

It was raining when the accident happened.
My friends were watching TV when the fire started.

GRAMMAR BUILDER 3

3B Quantity: *some, any, much, many*, etc.

1 Complete the sentences with *some* or *any*. → 3.1, 3.2

1 I need _____ fresh air.
2 There isn't _____ traffic on the road.
3 Are there _____ fields near your school?
4 Have you got _____ homework?
5 I'm going out with _____ friends.
6 We haven't got _____ pets.

2 Complete the sentences with *a little* or *a few*. → 3.3

1 'Would you like some pasta?' 'Just _____. I'm not very hungry.'
2 I went to the cinema with _____ friends last night.
3 I spent _____ time chatting with my uncle.
4 She bought _____ CDs in town.
5 I only recognised _____ people at the party.
6 She isn't a vegetarian, but she only eats _____ meat.

3 Complete the sentences with *much* or *many*. → 3.4, 3.6

1 There aren't _____ street lamps in my street.
2 Hurry up! We haven't got _____ time.
3 Has she got _____ friends at school?
4 Do you listen to _____ rap music?
5 He doesn't speak _____ German.
6 There aren't _____ cottages in the village.

4 Complete the sentences with *a lot of* and words from the box. → 3.5

countries	homework	goals	money	old people
traffic				

1 She's always buying expensive jewellery. She's got _____.
2 Sorry I'm late. There was _____ on the roads.
3 Did Chelsea score _____ in the match?
4 There are _____ in the town.
5 English is spoken in _____.
6 I can't go out tonight. Our teacher gave us _____.

3D Articles

5 Complete the sentences with *a* or *the*. → 3.7

1 My dad's got _____ BMW and my mum's got _____ Volkswagen. _____ BMW is much faster than _____ Volkswagen.
2 I met _____ girl and _____ boy at the party. _____ girl was from France, and _____ boy was from Spain.
3 She lives in _____ flat in the centre of town. _____ flat is very small.
4 There was _____ cinema and _____ disco in our town, but _____ cinema closed last year.
5 There's _____ bus at 10 or _____ train at 11. _____ bus arrives at 12, _____ train arrives at 11.30.
6 'I'd like _____ pizza and _____ piece of chocolate cake.' 'Would you like chips with _____ pizza?'
7 I bought _____ Madonna CD and _____ Robbie Williams CD. _____ Madonna CD was OK, but I didn't like _____ Robbie Williams album.

6 Complete each pair of sentences with *a* and *the*. → 3.8, 3.9

1 a There's _____ clothes shop near the post office.
  b I love _____ clothes shop between the bank and the chemist's.
2 a Shut _____ door, please.
  b My bedroom has got _____ blue door.
3 a I like this song. Who's _____ singer?
  b I think Anastacia is _____ great singer.
4 a Sandra's _____ lovely girl.
  b Who's _____ girl with long dark hair?
5 a Look. There's _____ cat in that tree.
  b 'Which cat is yours?' '_____ black one.'
6 a Dad's watching television in _____ living room.
  b I'd like a house with _____ big living room.

7 Add *the* to the sentences. → 3.10

1 I saw President on TV last night.
2 I'd like to travel round world.
3 It was cold but sun was shining.
4 If you see an accident, you should phone police.
5 My brother wants to join army.
6 It's too cold to swim in sea.
7 Moon came out from behind the clouds.
8 Paris is capital of France.

8 Choose the correct answer. → 3.11

1 I hate **cold coffee / the cold coffee**.
2 'Where's **coffee / the coffee**?' 'It's in the cupboard.'
3 She loves **cats / the cats**.
4 I'm going to take **dogs / the dogs** for a walk.
5 I'm not very interested in **fashion / the fashion**.
6 My favourite sport is **football / the football**.
7 Where are **CDs / the CDs** that I bought yesterday?
8 We went swimming in the sea. **Water / The water** was really warm.

GRAMMAR REFERENCE 3

some and any

3.1

We usually use *some* in affirmative sentences and *any* in negative sentences and questions.

There are some traffic lights at the end of the road.
There's some pasta on the table.

The dog doesn't want any biscuits.
They haven't got any money.

Are there any cinemas in your town?
Do you need any help?

3.2

We usually use *some* when we offer or ask for something.

Would you like some tea?
Can I borrow some money?

a little, a few

3.3

We use *a little* with uncountable nouns. We use *a few* with countable nouns.

Julia ate a little rice.
Mike ate a few chips.

much, many and a lot of

3.4

We use *much*, *many* and *a lot of* to talk about quantity. We use *much* with uncountable nouns. We use *many* with countable nouns.

French people don't drink much tea.
Are there many pedestrian crossings in the town centre?

3.5

We use *a lot of* (or *lots of*) with countable and uncountable nouns.

Bill Gates has got a lot of/lots of money.
There are a lot of/lots of roadworks in London.

3.6

We often use *much* and *many* in negative sentences and questions. We don't often use them in affirmative sentences.

We didn't eat much food. **or** We didn't eat a lot of food.
Were there many people at the party? **or** Were there a lot of people at the party?

Charlotte's got a lot of money. ✓
Charlotte's got ~~much~~ money. ✗

Articles

3.7

We use *a* before singular countable nouns when we talk about something for the first time.
We use *the* when we talk about something again.

I've got a cat and a dog. The cat's called Joe and the dog's called Sally.
I had a pizza and a coffee. The pizza was great but the coffee was awful.

3.8

We use *the* when it is clear what we are talking about.

Mum's in the kitchen.   (the kitchen in our house)
The station is near the park.   (There's only one station and one park in our town.)
The man in the yellow jacket is my uncle.   (We know which man – he's wearing a yellow jacket.)

3.9

We use *a* when we say what somebody or something is.

Liverpool is a city in England.
Bob is a taxi driver.
Mozart was a great composer.

We use *a* when we say what somebody or something is like.

Scotland is a beautiful country.
That's a nice dress. Where did you buy it?
He's a good-looking young man.

3.10

We use *the* when there is only one of something.

the sun, the North Sea, the sky, the moon, the world

3.11

We don't use *the* when we are making generalisations.

I don't like classical music.
Fiona never drinks tea or coffee.

GRAMMAR BUILDER 4

4B Comparative and superlative adjectives

1 Write the comparative forms of the adjectives. → 4.1

1 large
2 tall
3 thin
4 early
5 good
6 easy
7 hot
8 bad

2 Complete the sentences with comparative adjectives from exercise 1. → 4.1

1 'Is Dave _____ than George?' 'Yes, he's 1m 85.'
2 This jacket is too small. Have you got a _____ one?
3 It isn't very warm today. It was much _____ yesterday.
4 Exams are _____ if you revise a lot.
5 Oh, dear, it's raining. We can't play tennis unless the weather gets _____.
6 I don't like Madonna's latest CDs. I prefer her _____ albums.
7 This pizza is too thick. I prefer _____ ones.
8 Mr Jones is a _____ teacher than Mr Smith. Mr Smith explains things more carefully.

3 Complete the sentences with the comparative form of the adjectives in brackets and *than*. → 4.1, 4.2

1 Do you think maths is _____ English? (difficult)
2 Science fiction films are _____ romantic comedies. (boring)
3 Real Madrid are a _____ football team _____ Liverpool. (successful)
4 Maria is _____ Joanna. (confident)
5 Historical dramas are _____ than war films. (entertaining)
6 Is football _____ ice hockey? (exciting)

4 Write sentences with superlative adjectives. → 4.4

1 chimpanzees / intelligent / animals / in the world
  Chimpanzees are the most intelligent animals in the world.
2 Mark / funny / boy / in the class
3 Russia / large / country / in the world
4 Hollywood films / popular films / in the world
5 Germany / has got / big / population / in Europe
6 who / hard-working / student / in the class?
7 *Schindler's List* / moving / film / I've ever seen

4D (not) as … as, too, enough

5 Write sentences with *as … as* and the adjective in brackets. → 4.3

1 The Robbie Williams CD and the Madonna CD both cost €15. (expensive)
  The Robbie Williams CD is as expensive as the Madonna CD.
2 Diana was born in 1960. Mike was born in 1960 too. (old)
3 Cathy and Joe both got top marks in the exam. (intelligent)
4 The BMW and the Mercedes both have a top speed of 200 km/h. (fast)
5 I'm very tired. You're very tired too. (tired)
6 I go swimming twice a week. You go swimming twice a week too. (often)

6 Rewrite the sentences with *not as … as*. → 4.3

1 Arnold Schwarzenegger is taller than Sylvester Stallone.
  Sylvester Stallone isn't as tall as Arnold Schwarzenegger.
2 Disaster films are more gripping than science fiction films.
3 *Friends* is funnier than *Malcolm in the Middle*.
4 The acting in *Gladiator* was better than the acting in *Troy*.
5 The cinema in the town is bigger than the cinema in the village.
6 I'm more interested in war films than you.

7 Complete the sentences with *too* and an adjective from the box. → 4.6

boring   cold   expensive   scary   sweet   tired   untidy

1 It's _____ in here to have the window open. Can you close it, please?
2 That CD is _____. It's €40.
3 I can't drink this tea. It's _____.
4 That film is _____ to watch from beginning to end.
5 I'm not going to stay up and watch the film with you. I'm _____.
6 I can't find anything in my room. It's _____.
7 I'm not going to watch the horror film with you. It's _____.

8 Complete the sentences with *enough* and a noun or adjective from the box. → 4.6, 4.7

exercise   funny   old   people   time   television

1 I haven't got _____ to finish my homework.
2 I didn't enjoy the comedy. It wasn't _____.
3 He doesn't do _____ to stay healthy.
4 We can't play football. There aren't _____.
5 I'm not _____ to drive a car.
6 Go to bed. You've watched _____.

Comparative adjectives

4.1

Spelling

We add *-er* to short (one-syllable and some two-syllable) adjectives.

+ *-er*   long → longer

If the short adjective ends in *-e*, we add *-r*.

+ *-r*   wide → wider

If the short adjective ends in a short vowel + a single consonant, we double the consonant and add *-er*.

-t → *-tter*   hot → hotter

If the adjective ends in *-y*, we take out the *-y* and add *-ier*.

-y → *-ier*   friendly → friendlier

If the adjective is long (two syllables or more), we use the word *more*.

gripping → more gripping

Some adjectives have irregular comparative forms.

good → better
bad → worse
far → further

than

4.2

We use *than* to compare two things or people.
Bowfinger was funnier than The Nutty Professor.

We usually use the object pronoun (*me, you, her, him, us, them*) after *than*.
You're taller than me. ✓
You're taller than I. ✗
but You're taller than I am. ✓

(not) as ... as

4.3

We use *(not) as ... as* to compare two people or things.

not as ... as means *less ... than*.
Jude Law is not as old as Brad Pitt. Brad Pitt was born in 1963, Jude Law in 1972.

as ... as means *equally ...*
Sharon Stone is as tall as Tom Cruise. Sharon Stone and Tom Cruise are both 170 centimetres.

We usually use the object pronoun after *(not) as ... as*. The subject pronoun sounds very formal.
Sarah's as intelligent as him. ✓
Sarah's as intelligent as he. ✗
but Sarah's as intelligent as he is. ✓

Superlative adjectives

4.4

Spelling

We put *the* in front of short (one-syllable and some two-syllable) adjectives and add *-est*.

+ *-est*   long → the longest

If the short adjective ends in *-e*, we add *-st*.

+ *-st*   wide → the widest

If the short adjective ends in a short vowel + a single consonant, we double the consonant and add *-est*.

-t → *-ttest*   hot → the hottest

If the adjective ends in *-y*, we take out the *-y* and add *-iest*.

-y → *-iest*   friendly → the friendliest

If the adjective is long (two syllables or more), we use the word *most*.

gripping → the most gripping

Some adjectives have irregular superlative forms.

good → the best
bad → the worst
far → the furthest

less and *the least*

4.5

less and *the least* have the opposite meaning to *more* and *the most*.
Maths is less difficult than English.
What's the least interesting subject that you study?

too and *enough*

4.6

too comes before an adjective.
enough comes after an adjective.
This jacket is too small for him.
This jacket isn't big enough for him.

4.7

enough comes before a noun.
He can't buy it. He hasn't got enough money.

GRAMMAR BUILDER 5

5B Present perfect

1 Complete the phone conversation with the present perfect form of the verbs in brackets or short answers. → 5.1, 5.2, 5.3

Kate Hello, Kate speaking.

Dave Hi, Kate. It's David. I'm phoning from Budapest.

Kate Hi David! It's great to hear from you. So, you ¹_____ (find) your mobile!

Dave Actually, no. I ²_____ (buy) a new one, but my number ³_____ (not change).

Kate Well, it's great to hear from you. We ⁴_____ (not speak) for ages. ⁵_____ (you / find) somewhere to live yet?

Dave No, I ⁶_____, but I ⁷_____ (just / look) at a beautiful flat near the Danube.

Kate Are you going to live there?

Dave I ⁸_____ (not decide) yet. I can't really afford it!

Kate ⁹_____ (you start) work?

Dave Yes, I ¹⁰_____. I ¹¹_____ (give) about twenty lessons, but the school ¹²_____ (not pay) me yet!

2 What have or haven't you done today? Write an affirmative and a negative sentence in the present perfect for each verb in the box. → 5.1, 5.2, 5.3

eat   drink   hear   see   speak

3 Complete the sentences with *been* or *gone*. → 5.4

1 'Where's Maria?' 'She's _____ to the supermarket.'

2 Jake has _____ to the shops. Look at all the CDs he has bought.

3 'Are you going to the Picasso exhibition in London?' 'I've already _____ to it. It was fantastic.'

4 Tom has _____ to Jim's for lunch. He'll be back about two.

5 'I want to speak to Jill. Has she _____ yet?' 'No, she's still here.'

4 Choose *for* or *since*. → 5.3

1 My grandparents have been married **for / since** 40 years.

2 It hasn't snowed here **for / since** 1998.

3 He's had a girlfriend **for / since** last summer.

4 They've been engaged **for / since** twelve years.

5 I've been in love with Britney **for / since** I was twelve years old.

6 You haven't phoned me **for / since** ages.

5 Write questions with *How long ...?* and answers with *for* or *since*. → 5.5

1 I'm a teacher. I started teaching last year.
   How long have you been a teacher?
   Since last year. / For a year.

2 I live near the coast. I moved there three years ago.

3 I'm married. I got married two years ago.

4 I know Mary. We first met last Christmas.

5 I work in a factory. I started working there in 1994.

6 I play the piano. I had my first lesson in 2001.

7 I've got a passport. I got it three years ago.

5D Present perfect and past simple

6 Complete the conversations with the verbs in the boxes. Use the past simple or present perfect form. → 5.6, 5.7

go   stay   visit

Harry ¹_____ you _____ to the USA?

Fiona Yes, I ²_____ San Francisco last year.

Harry Where ³_____ you _____?

Fiona At my uncle's house.

be   give   open   receive   say   write

Harry ⁴_____ you _____ a present that you didn't like?

Fiona Yes, my aunt ⁵_____ me a yellow sweatshirt for my birthday.

Harry What ⁶_____ you _____ to her?

Fiona Nothing. She ⁷_____ there when I _____ it. But I ⁸_____ her a nice thank-you letter.

7 Write questions with *Have you ever ...?*. Write true answers about yourself. If the answer is yes, add more details in the past simple. → 5.6, 5.7

1 go / snowboarding
   Have you ever been snowboarding?
   No, I haven't.
   Yes, I have. I went snowboarding in Zakopane last winter.

2 go / to France or Switzerland

3 swim / in the sea

4 break / a bone

5 play / a computer game

6 borrow / money from a friend

7 visit / a museum

8 Some of the sentences are incorrect. Rewrite them using the correct tense. → 5.6, 5.7

1 I've been to London yesterday.
   I went to London yesterday.

2 She's written three e-mails last night.

3 Last summer we saw some beautiful lakes in Italy.

4 Have you ever met anyone famous?

5 Last Christmas my parents have given me an MP3 player.

6 I lived in London since last year.

7 'Did you buy any presents yet?' 'No, not yet.'

8 'Have you ever been snorkelling?' 'Yes, I've been snorkelling last summer.'

GRAMMAR REFERENCE (5)

Present perfect

5.1

We form the present perfect like this:

Affirmative	
I've finished	we've finished
you've finished	you've finished
he/she/it's finished	they've finished

Short form and full form	
I've = I have	
she's = she has	

Negative	
I haven't finished	we haven't finished
you haven't finished	you haven't finished
he/she/it hasn't finished	they haven't finished

Short form and full form	
haven't = have not	
hasn't = has not	

Interrogative	
Have I finished ...?	Have we finished ...?
Have you finished ...?	Have you finished ...?
Has he/she/it finished ...?	Have they finished ...?

Short answer	
Yes, I have. / No, I haven't.	
Yes, she has. / No, she hasn't.	

5.2

We form the present perfect with the present tense of the auxiliary verb *have* and the past participle.
Pete has finished his homework.

The past participle of regular verbs is the same as the past simple.
played   danced   studied   dropped

Sometimes irregular verbs have the same past participle as the past simple form, sometimes they are different.
buy – bought – bought
see – saw – seen

For a list of irregular verbs see the Workbook.

5.3

We use the present perfect:
- to talk about recent events.
  Pete has passed all his exams.
- to talk about experiences.
  I've eaten snails in France.
- to talk about an event or situation that began in the past and continues up to now. We use *for* with a period of time and *since* with a point in time.
  My dad has worked for IBM for 10 years.
  I've had this MP3 player since May.
- to talk about actions that have an effect on the present.
  I haven't finished my homework, so I can't go out.

5.4

We use both *been* and *gone* as the past participles of the verb *go*. We use *been* when somebody has returned.
John has been shopping. (He went shopping but he is here now.)
We use *gone* when somebody hasn't returned.
John has gone shopping. (He went shopping and he is still at the shops.)

5.5

We use *How long ...?* and the present perfect to ask how long a situation has continued up to the present.
'How long have you lived in London?' 'Since 2001.'

Present perfect and past simple

See the Workbook for the forms of the past simple.

5.6

We use both the past simple and the present perfect to talk about finished actions.

We use the past simple to talk about completed events at a definite time in the past. The events have no connection with the present.
I visited the USA last year.

We use the present perfect to talk about past events that have a connection with the present. See point 5.3 for a list of the uses of the present perfect.

5.7

We often use the past simple when we ask for or give more details following a *Have you ever ...?* question.
Have you ever been to a pop concert?
Yes, I have. I went to a Robbie Williams concert last year.

Have you ever been skiing?
Yes, I have.
Where did you go?
I went to Zakopane.

GRAMMAR BUILDER 6

6B *will* and *going to*

1 Write predictions about technology in ten years' time. Use *I think …* or *I don't think …* and the phrases in the box. → 6.1, 6.2

> all children / have a mobile phone
> camcorders / be very small
> digital cameras / be very expensive
> cars / need petrol
> houses / use solar energy
> watches / include MP3 players

I think all children will have a mobile phone.

2 Think of offers or promises for the problems in the box. Use *I'll …*. → 6.1, 6.2

> I can't do my homework.
> I need to call my mum, but I haven't got my mobile phone.
> I want to watch this film, but my DVD player is broken.
> I'm going to miss my favourite TV programme tonight.

3 **SPEAKING** Work in pairs. Student A: describe a problem from exercise 2. Student B: Offer or promise to do something.

> I can't do my homework.

> I'll ask my sister to help you.

4 Match the pairs of sentences. → 6.1, 6.2

1 'What would you like to eat, sir?'
2 'Have you got Sam's number?'
3 'These pens are 90p each.'
4 'The shower isn't working.'
5 'We're leaving now.'

a 'I'm not sure. I'll look in my phonebook.'
b 'I'll go with you.'
c 'I'll have the pasta, please.'
d 'I'll have a bath.'
e 'I'll take three.'

5 Write predictions about the pictures with *going to*. Use the verbs in the box to help you. → 6.3, 6.4

> chase   crash   fall off   fall over   frighten   scream   steal

6 Write down three things you intend to do this weekend and three things you don't intend to do. Use *I'm (not) going to … .* → 6.3, 6.4

I'm not going to do any homework.

6D Zero conditional / *may, might, could*

7 Match the two halves of the sentences. → 6.6

1 If you press this button,
2 If you can't say anything nice,
3 I'm here
4 If I drink coffee in the evening,
5 It doesn't matter
6 If you say 'sit',

a if you need me.
b if you break that calculator – it was cheap.
c I never sleep well.
d the lights come on.
e my dog sits down.
f don't say anything at all.

8 Complete the text with *may*, *might* and *could* and the verbs in the box. There is one negative form.

> become   do   happen   prefer   share   want

Sales of CDs are declining because of illegal file sharing, and film companies are worried that the same thing ^{1}_____ with DVDs. As downloads become faster, more and more people ^{2}_____ films over the Internet rather than buying them. Buying DVDs ^{3}_____ a thing of the past. The music industry now encourages legal downloads from websites like the iTunes Music Store. The film industry ^{4}_____ something similar. However, if they try to charge too much for film downloads, people ^{5}_____ to pay. They ^{6}_____ to download them illegally using one of the many file-sharing programs.

GRAMMAR REFERENCE 6

will

6.1

We use *will* to talk about the future. We form sentences with *will* like this:
* *will* + infinitive without *to*
  I will go.

The form of *will* is the same for all persons (*I*, *you*, *he*, *she*, etc.).

Affirmative
I'll see you later.
She'll be angry.
(full form = *will*)

Negative
I won't tell anybody.
They won't listen to you.
(full form = *will not*)

Interrogative
Will you be at home?
Will it work?

Short answer
Yes, I will.
No, it won't.

6.2

We use *will*:
* to make factual statements about the future.
  There will be a solar eclipse in 2026.
* to make predictions, especially when they are based on our own thoughts or beliefs.
  I think you'll do well in your exams.
  I don't think England will win the next World Cup.
* to make offers.
  I'll carry your bags.
  I'll lend you my phone.
* to make promises.
  I'll always love you.
* to make instant decisions (decisions that we make while we are speaking).
  Look! There's Tommy. I'll go and say hello.

going to

6.3

We use *be going to* to talk about the future. We form sentences with *be going to* like this:
* present simple of *be* + *going to* + infinitive without *to*
  I'm going to take my driving test next year.
  Roger Federer isn't going to win the match.
  Are you going to be at home this weekend?
  Yes, I am. / No, I'm not.

6.4

We use *be going to*:
* to make predictions, especially when they are based on what we can see.
  Look at that man! He's going to jump in the river!
* to talk about our intentions.
  I'm going to invite her to my party.

6.5

We use both *will* and *be going to* to make predictions and to talk about our decisions. However, we use them in a slightly different way.

We use ...	will	be going to
predictions	based on our own knowledge and opinions: Rooney will score. He always scores in important games.	based on the situation and what we can see: Rooney's got the ball! He's going to score!
decisions	instant decisions that we make while speaking: Show me the menu. Hmm. I'll have chicken.	intentions – things that we have already decided: I'm going to have chicken tonight. I bought it this morning.

Zero conditional

6.6

We use the zero conditional to talk about a result which follows a particular action. We use the present simple to describe the action and the present simple to describe the result.
If you press this button, the light comes on.
The *if* clause can come before or after the main clause. If it comes after, we don't use a comma.
If you heat ice, it melts.
Ice melts if you heat it.

7B   *must*, *mustn't* and *needn't*

1 Match the pairs of sentences. → 7.1, 7.2

1 You mustn't eat those mushrooms.
2 You must drive on the left.
3 You mustn't swim here.
4 You must pay for those books.
5 You mustn't worry about your exams.
6 You must try on that top.

a You're in England!
b You don't want to buy the wrong size.
c They're poisonous.
d They'll be fine.
e They aren't free.
f The river is dangerous.

2 What do the signs mean? Complete the sentences with *must* or *mustn't*. → 7.1, 7.2

 1 You <u>mustn't</u> turn left.

 2 You _____ stop here.

 3 You _____ smoke.

 4 You _____ switch off your mobile phone.

 5 You _____ be eighteen to see this film.

 6 You _____ dive here.

 7 You _____ wear a hard hat.

 8 You _____ turn right.

3 Rewrite the sentences using *needn't*. → 7.3

1 It isn't necessary for you to buy her a present.
   You needn't buy her a present.

2 It isn't necessary for us to arrive on time.
3 It isn't necessary for them to phone me.
4 It isn't necessary for him to wear a suit.
5 It isn't necessary for her to cook dinner for me.
6 It isn't necessary for you to wait for me.

7D   First conditional

4 Match the two halves of the sentences. → 7.4, 7.5

1 If I don't go to bed soon, …
2 I won't pass my exam …
3 My brother will help me …
4 If you have a party, …
5 We won't have a barbecue …
6 Will your brother be angry …

a … will you invite me?
b … I'll be tired tomorrow.
c … if we use his computer?
d … if my homework is too difficult.
e … if it rains tomorrow.
f … if I don't study hard.

5 Complete the first conditional sentences with the present simple form of the words in brackets. → 7.4, 7.5

1 If he _____ (eat) too much, he won't sleep well.
2 I'll feed his cat while he's away if he _____ (ask) me.
3 We won't get home before it's dark if we _____ (leave) after 5.30 p.m.
4 If you _____ (work) harder, you'll do better at school.
5 If it _____ (snow) next month, we'll go skiing.
6 She'll be angry if he _____ (not come) to her party.

6 Complete the first conditional sentences with the *will* form of the words in brackets. → 7.4, 7.5

1 If you give me your number, I _____ (call) you tomorrow.
2 They _____ (not buy) a new car if it costs too much.
3 If you don't tell your parents where you are, they _____ (be) worried.
4 You _____ (have) a great time if you come to the party.
5 What _____ you _____ (do) if it rains tomorrow?
6 If we can't find a hotel, where _____ we _____ ? (sleep)

GRAMMAR REFERENCE 7

must and mustn't

7.1

The form of *must* or *mustn't* is the same for all persons (*I*, *you*, *he*, etc.).

Affirmative
I must go home.
You must tell the truth.

Negative
You mustn't tell anybody.
They mustn't be late.
(full form = must not)

Interrogative*
Must you leave so early?

Short answer
Yes, I must.

* We don't often make questions with *must*. It is more common to use *Do you have to ...?*

7.2

We use *must* + infinitive without *to* to say that something is necessary, and it is very important to do it.

In some Asian countries, you must eat with your right hand.

You must be quiet in the school library.

We use *mustn't* + infinitive without *to* to say that something is prohibited, and it is very important not to do it.

We mustn't be late for school.

You mustn't use a mobile phone in the cinema.

We often use *must* or *mustn't* to express rules and laws.

In the UK, you must be 17 to drive a car.

You mustn't smoke on aeroplanes.

needn't

7.3

We use *needn't* + infinitive without *to* to say that something is not necessary but isn't against the rules.

You needn't bring a towel. There are towels at the swimming pool. *(But you can bring one if you want.)*

You needn't take sandwiches as lunch is provided. *(But you can bring them if you want.)*

First conditional

7.4

We use the first conditional to predict the result of a future action. We use the present simple to describe the action and *will* + infinitive without *to* to describe the result.

If you go to bed late, you'll be tired tomorrow.
　　(action)　　　　(result)

If I miss the bus, I'll take a taxi.
　　(action)　　(result)

7.5

The *if* clause can come before or after the main clause. If it comes after, we don't use a comma.

If you drink too much coffee, you won't sleep well.

You won't sleep well if you drink too much coffee.

8B Second conditional

1 Complete the sentences with the past simple form of the verbs in brackets. → 8.1, 8.2

1 If I (have) _____ a bicycle, I'd ride to school.
2 If I (owe) _____ money to my parents, I'd pay them back.
3 He'd write more often if he (have) _____ more time.
4 If I (know) _____ the answer, I'd tell you.
5 If we (not live) _____ in the city, I'd get really bored.
6 Would you be angry if I (copy) _____ your homework?
7 You wouldn't be so tired in the mornings if you (not stay up) _____ so late.
8 If Pete (not smoke) _____, he'd be much healthier.

2 Complete the second conditional sentences with the correct form of the verbs in brackets. → 8.1, 8.2

1 If they (live) _____ in the city, life (be) _____ easier.
2 I (play) _____ basketball if I (be) _____ taller.
3 If we (have) _____ a DVD player, we (watch) _____ films every evening.
4 You (can) _____ afford that MP3 player if you (not spend) _____ all your money on clothes.
5 What (happen) _____ if you (not go) _____ to school tomorrow?
6 He (not be) _____ very happy if you (not invite) _____ him to your birthday party.
7 If I (find) _____ a credit card, I (take) _____ it to the police.
8 How (you / feel) _____ if you (not pass) _____ your exams?

3 Write second conditional sentences. → 8.1, 8.2

1 I don't have a computer, so I don't play computer games.
   If I had a computer, I'd play computer games.
2 Ben has to get up early on Mondays, so he doesn't go out on Sunday evenings.
3 Kate doesn't have a ticket for the Madonna concert, so she isn't going.
4 There isn't a football match on TV this evening, so they're going out.
5 I have a lot of homework, so I'll stay in this evening.
6 We don't have to help with the cooking, so we can watch a DVD.

8D I wish ...

4 Write the sentences in the correct speech bubbles. → 8.3, 8.4

I wish I could buy that jacket.
I wish I lived in the country.
I wish I were taller.
I wish the music wasn't so loud.
I wish we had tickets.
I wish you could talk.

5 Complete the sentences with the correct form of the verbs in brackets. → 8.3, 8.4

1 I wish I _____ (not have) so much homework.
2 I wish we _____ (be) in the same class.
3 Jim wishes he _____ (can) dance.
4 I wish it _____ (not be) winter.
5 Patricia wishes she _____ (not hate) pizza.
6 I'm having a great time in Majorca. I wish you _____ (be) here.
7 I wish I _____ (can) eat bread, but I can't.
8 I wish I _____ (not have to) take an exam at the end of the year.

GRAMMAR REFERENCE 8

Second conditional

8.1

We use the second conditional to talk about situations that are unlikely or unreal. It can refer to the present or the future.

We use the past tense to describe the unlikely, unreal or imaginary action or situation, and *would* + infinitive without *to* to describe the result.

If I had a lot of money, I'd visit the USA.

8.2

The *if* clause can come before or after the main clause. If it comes after, we don't use a comma.

If I lived in the country, I'd have a dog.
I'd have a dog if I lived in the country.

I wish ...

8.3

We use *wish* + past simple or past continuous to say that we want something to be different from how it is now.

The present situation: Alison has brown eyes.
Wish: Alison wishes she had blue eyes.
The present situation: It's cold. I am wearing a jacket.
Wish: I wish I was wearing a coat.

8.4

After *if* and *wish* we sometimes use *were* rather than *was* with *I/he/she/it*. *Were* is more formal than *was*.

GRAMMAR BUILDER 9

9B Past perfect

1 Complete the sentences with the past perfect form of the verbs in brackets. → 9.1, 9.2

1 I didn't watch the film because I _____ (see) it.
2 She felt ill because she _____ (eat) too much.
3 We couldn't drive to Liverpool because our car _____ (break down).
4 He _____ (not finish) his homework so he couldn't go out.
5 'Why was he so hungry?' 'Because he _____ (not have) lunch.'
6 I _____ (buy) the tickets before I heard you were ill.
7 He couldn't go out because he _____ (promise) to help his mum with the housework.
8 Last year I went to San Francisco. I _____ (not visit) the USA before.
9 After I _____ (write) the letter, I posted it.
10 When dad _____ (do) the gardening, he watched TV.

2 Write one sentence, using the past simple and the past perfect. Start with *When*. → 9.1, 9.2

1 Joe went out. I arrived home.
   When I arrived home, Joe had gone out.
2 I went to bed. Paul phoned.
   When Paul ...
3 The shoplifter ran away. The police arrived.
4 Dad cooked dinner. Mum got home.
5 The vandals sprayed graffiti on the wall. The police caught them.
6 The film started. We arrived at the cinema.
7 It started to rain. We left the beach.
8 The train left. We got to the station.

9D Reported speech

3 Complete the sentences in reported speech. Use the past simple, past continuous or past perfect. → 9.3, 9.4

1 'I like pizza,' said Fred.
   Fred said that he liked pizza.
2 'A shoplifter stole three CDs,' said the shop assistant.
   The shop assistant said that a shoplifter _____ three CDs.
3 'Drug dealers are selling drugs in front of my house,' the man said.
   The man said that drug dealers _____ drugs in front of his house.
4 'It's getting dark,' said Jess.
   Jess said that it _____ dark.
5 'Some vandals smashed the shop window,' she said.
   She said that some vandals _____ the shop window.
6 'The burglar is in the police car,' said the police officer.
   The police officer said that the burglar _____ in the police car.
7 'Two men robbed the bank,' the bank manager said.
   The bank manager said that two men _____ the bank.
8 'Every day joyriders steal ten cars in the city,' said the police officer.
   The police officer said that every day joyriders _____ ten cars in the city.

4 Complete the sentences with the correct pronoun. → 9.4

1 'I'm going home,' said Cathy.
   Cathy said that _____ was going home.
2 'We live in Birmingham,' she said.
   She said that _____ lived in Birmingham.
3 'I like watching TV in my bedroom,' he said.
   He said that _____ liked watching TV in _____ bedroom.
4 'You're late!' she said to me.
   She said to _____ that _____ was late.
5 'He never phones me,' said Elizabeth.
   Elizabeth said that _____ never phoned _____.

5 Rewrite what Fiona says using reported speech. → 9.3, 9.4

1 I'm hungry. Fiona said that she was hungry.

2 I didn't have any breakfast. _____

3 I want a banana. _____

4 I'm going out. _____

5 My friend is meeting me at the cinema. _____

6 My friend's name is Tom. _____

7 I first met him last year. _____

8 We're going to see a Johnny Depp film. _____

6 Rewrite the sentences in direct speech. → 9.3, 9.4

1 He said that it wasn't raining.
   'It isn't raining,' he said.
2 She said that last month joyriders had stolen her car.
3 He said that he needed a holiday.
4 You said that you were going to Tom's party this evening.
5 He said that he'd seen the robbers leaving the bank.
6 She said that I was greedy.
7 You said that you'd had lunch.
8 He said that he was feeling ill.

GRAMMAR REFERENCE 9

Past perfect

9.1

We form the past perfect like this:

Affirmative
I/you'd gone
he/she/it'd gone
we/you/they'd gone

Short form and full form
'd = had

Negative
I/you hadn't gone
he/she/it hadn't gone
we/you/they hadn't gone

Short form and full form
hadn't = had not

Interrogative
Had I/you gone ...?
Had he/she/it gone ...?
Had we/you/they gone ...?

Short answer
Yes, I had. / No, I hadn't.
Yes, she had. / No, she hadn't.

The past participle of regular verbs is the same as the past simple.

finished   danced   studied   chatted

Sometimes irregular verbs have the same past participle as the past simple form, sometimes they are different.

go – went – been/gone
buy – bought – bought
see – saw – seen

For a list of irregular verbs see the Workbook.

9.2

We use the past perfect to talk about an event in the past which happened before another event in the past.

Time line

the robbers left the bank   the police arrived   Now

When the police arrived, the robbers had left the bank.

Reported speech

9.3

When we report somebody else's words, the tense of the verb usually changes.

Direct speech	Reported speech
Present simple →	Past simple
'I don't like dogs,' Ben said.	Ben said (that) he didn't like dogs.
'My dad is at work,' Becky said.	Becky said that her dad was at work.
Present continuous →	Past continuous
'He's wearing a blue top,' Michelle said.	Michelle said (that) he was wearing a blue top.
Past simple →	Past perfect
'We moved to London in 2000,' Phil said.	Phil said (that) they had moved to London in 2000.

It is not necessary to use *that* in reported speech.

9.4

The pronouns sometimes change, depending on the context.

'My name's Jill,' she said.
She said that **her** name was Jill.

'We went to the cinema,' Mark said.
Mark said that **they** had gone to the cinema.

'I'll meet you after school,' Becky said.
Becky said **she**'d meet **me** after school.

GRAMMAR BUILDER 10

10B The passive (present simple)

1 Complete the sentences with the present simple passive form of the verbs in brackets. → 10.1, 10.2, 10.3

1 Rice _____ (grow) in China.
2 Helmets _____ (wear) by ice hockey players.
3 Spanish _____ (speak) in Mexico.
4 Coffee _____ (drink) in most countries of the world.
5 English _____ (teach) in schools all over Europe.
6 Turkey _____ (eat) at Christmas.

2 Complete the text with the present simple passive form of the verbs in brackets. → 10.1, 10.2, 10.3

Celebrity Magazine Interviews

First, the celebrity [1] _____ (contact) by the magazine. If the celebrity agrees to the interview, a reporter [2] _____ (send) to their house. The celebrity [3] _____ (interview) and lots of photographs [4] _____ (take). Then the article [5] _____ (write) — it's always a very kind one — and a lot of money [6] _____ (pay) to the celebrity!

3 Complete the sentences with the present simple passive form of the verbs in the box. → 10.1, 10.2, 10.3

eat   grow   make   sell   send   speak   visit

1 Tea _____ in India.
2 Newspapers and magazines _____ in a newsagent's.
3 English _____ in Australia and New Zealand.
4 The best chocolate _____ in Belgium and Switzerland.
5 In the UK too many criminals _____ to prison.
6 Every year, 38 billion burgers _____ in the USA.
7 Every year Paris _____ by 24 million tourists.

4 Rewrite the sentences in the passive. → 10.1, 10.2, 10.3

1 They recycle a lot of paper and cardboard in Britain.
2 They don't sell books in this shop.
3 They don't make Camembert cheese in Germany.
4 They use recycled paper in newspapers.
5 They don't grow oranges in Hungary.
6 They don't drink alcohol in some Muslim countries.

10D The passive (other tenses)

5 Complete the sentences with the past simple passive form of the verbs in brackets. → 10.4

1 This DVD player _____ (make) in Korea.
2 *The Lord of the Rings* _____ (write) by J.R.R. Tolkien.
3 Jeans _____ (invent) in the USA.
4 Shakespeare's plays _____ (perform) for the first time about 400 years ago.
5 John Lennon _____ (murder) in New York in 1980.
6 Pluto _____ (discover) in 1930.

6 Rewrite the sentences in the passive. Use *by* if necessary to say who has done the action. → 10.3, 10.4

1 Somebody has stolen my camera.
2 Somebody has vandalised the bus stop.
3 Shoplifters have taken the new DVDs.
4 Somebody has burgled their house.
5 They've murdered three people.
6 The police have interviewed three suspects.

7 Complete the advertisement with the passive form of *will*.

Car Valet Service!

Your car [1] _____ (collect) from your home. It [2] _____ (clean) by hand, and the doors and windows [3] _____ (polish). Any rubbish [4] _____ (take) out of the car and the seats [5] _____ (hoover). The car [6] _____ (return) to you the same day!

GRAMMAR REFERENCE 10

Passive (present simple)

10.1

We form the present simple passive like this:
- present simple of *be* + past participle of the main verb.

Affirmative
This newspaper is published daily.
These grapes are grown in Italy.

Negative
This wine isn't made in France.
Cars aren't used on the island of Tresco.

Interrogative
Is your bicycle serviced regularly?
Are your clothes washed by hand?

Short answer
Yes, it is. / No, it isn't.
Yes, they are. / No, they aren't.

10.2

We use the passive when we want to focus on the action, not on who performs it, or when we don't know who performs it.
We often use the present simple passive to describe a process.
First, the bottles are washed. Then they're sorted into different colours. Next, they ..., etc.

10.3

When we want to say who performed the action, we use *by*.
My exams are marked by the teachers.

Passive (other tenses)

10.4

We form other tenses of the passive like this:
- correct tense of *be* + past participle of the main verb.

Tense	Example
past simple	This house **was built** in 1850.
	My friends **were robbed** in Mexico last year.
present perfect	Our car **has been stolen**!
	The Harry Potter books **have been read** by millions.
will (future simple)	His first novel **will be published** next year.
	The pyramids **will be closed** next week.

VOCABULARY BUILDER 1

PART 1

1 Label the pictures with the adjectives in the box.

> friendly   funny   hard-working   kind   lazy   rude
> shy   talkative

2 Choose the correct adjectives.

1 He's **kind / unkind**. He never helps people.
2 He's **optimistic / pessimistic**. He always thinks bad things are going to happen.
3 She's **patient / impatient**. She doesn't mind waiting.
4 He's **funny / serious**. He always tells jokes.
5 She's **generous / mean**. She always spends money on other people.

3 Rewrite the sentences in exercise 2 so that they mean the opposite.

1 He's kind. He always helps people.

4 SPEAKING Work in pairs. Ask and answer questions about your personalities.

> Are you kind?

> Yes, I am. Are you confident?

> No, I'm not. I'm shy.

PART 2

Negative prefixes: *un-*, *im- / in-* and *dis-*

> **Look out!**
>
> *negative prefixes*
> The prefixes *un-*, *in-* (or *im-*) and *dis-* are negative. When they come before an adjective, they make its meaning opposite.
> *kind – unkind*   *patient – impatient*   *honest – dishonest*

5 Read the definitions. Complete the definitions for the opposites.

1 An honest person always tells the truth.
   A dishonest person …
2 An ambitious person tries very hard to be successful.
   An unambitious person …
3 A polite person is never rude.
   An impolite person …
4 A tidy person always puts things away.
   An untidy person …
5 A loyal person is your friend for a long time.
   A disloyal person …
6 A tolerant person listens to other people's opinions.
   An intolerant person …
7 An active person gets a lot of exercise.
   An inactive person …
8 A lucky person usually has good luck.
   An unlucky person …

6 Complete the sentences. Use the adjectives in the box, with or without the prefix *un-*.

> attractive   believable   certain   comfortable   fit
> grateful

1 He's very _____. He could be a model or a film star.
2 She's very _____. She can run 10 kilometres.
3 I can't sleep. This bed is very _____.
4 Thanks for the present. I'm very _____.
5 England are beating Brazil 8-0. That's _____!
6 He's definitely rich. I'm _____.

VOCABULARY BUILDER **2**

PART 1

1 What are the people doing? Use the correct verb: *play*, *go* or *do*.

She's doing athletics.

2 Match the sports in the box with the pictures.

| badminton | basketball | golf | ice hockey | rugby |
| weightlifting | | | | |

3 What do you think? Put the sports in the box in order from 1 (most interesting) to 6 (least interesting).

| football | gymnastics | judo | swimming | tennis |
| volleyball | | | | |

4 SPEAKING Work in pairs. Ask and answer questions to find out what your partner thinks.

What do you think of ...?

I love it. / I like it. / It's OK. / I'm not very interested in it. / I hate it.

PART 2

Collocations: sports and games

5 Read the sentences. Complete the chart with the words from the box.

'We scored eight points in ten minutes, but we didn't win the game.'

'John passed the ball to me and I kicked it, but I missed the goal. Because of that we lost the match.'

| kick | lose | miss | pass | score | win |

Verbs	Nouns
compete in / lose / win	a race
_____ / win	a match
lose / _____	a game
lose / _____ / win	a point
_____ / score	a goal
miss / score	a penalty
hit / _____ / _____ / throw	a ball

6 Look at the pictures. What are the people doing? Use noun and verb collocations from exercise 5.

He's competing in a race.

PART 1

1 Complete the sentences with some of the words from the box.

> advertisement bus stop cottage field footpath gate
> hedge hill lane pavement pedestrian crossing
> postbox road sign roadworks rubbish bin stream
> street lamps traffic lights village wood

1 Don't throw that paper on the ground. Put it in the
   _____.
2 Walk on the _____, not in the road.
3 The _____ were red so the car stopped.
4 'What does that _____ mean?' 'It means that cars
   can't go down that street.'
5 We walked along a _____ to the top of a hill.
6 This street is very dark. They should put up some
   _____.
7 Sarah lives in a white _____ in a small village.
8 Close the _____ behind you or the cows will
   follow us out of the _____.
9 It's dangerous to cross the street here. Use the
   _____.
10 Can you put this letter in the _____ for me?
11 The _____ has got a population of 1,500.

2 Match the description with one of the pictures a, b or c.

There's a pedestrian crossing and some traffic lights. A man
is standing on the pavement near the traffic lights. There
aren't many cars. On the right there's a bus stop with an
advertisement. On the left there's a postbox.

3 SPEAKING Work in pairs. Describe one of the other pictures.
Your partner says which picture.

> On the left there's a postbox.

> Is it picture b?

> Yes, it is.

PART 2

Extension: compound nouns

4 Study the information in the *Learn this!* box. Find eight more
compound nouns in the box in exercise 1.

LEARN THIS!

1 We can form compound nouns from two nouns.
2 We usually write them as two words (e.g. post office),
   but sometimes as one word (e.g. postbox). You need
   to check in a dictionary.

5 Match each noun 1–10 with a noun a–j to make compound
nouns. (Four of them are written as one word.)

1	basket_____	a	teacher
2	swimming_____	b	work
3	week_____	c	tennis
4	home_____	d	pool
5	sweat_____	e	shirt
6	shopping_____	f	end
7	head_____	g	game
8	pop_____	h	ball
9	computer_____	i	centre
10	table_____	j	music

Look out!   *stress in two-word compound nouns*
The main stress is usually on the first word (e.g. *post office*)
but sometimes the stress is on both words (e.g.
pedestrian crossing).

6 🎧 1.31 Listen and repeat the compound nouns from
exercise 5. Underline the stress.

7 Complete the sentences with the compound nouns from
exercise 5.

1 There's a really good _____ in the town centre.
   You can buy almost anything there.
2 'Where did you learn to swim?' 'I had lessons at the
   _____.'
3 Is the _____ of your school a man or a woman?
4 'What are you doing at the _____?' 'I'm going to
   stay with my cousin.'
5 Our teachers gave us a lot of _____ last night. It
   took me three hours to finish it.
6 If you're hot, take off your _____.
7 I played _____ with my sister this morning. She
   won 21–18.
8 I think the Chicago Bulls is the best _____ team
   in the USA.
9 I never listen to _____ on the radio.
10 'Is Tom watching TV?' 'No, he's playing a _____ in
   his bedroom.'

VOCABULARY BUILDER 4

PART 1

1 Think of examples of all the types of film in the box.

> action film   animated film   comedy   disaster film
> historical drama   horror film   musical
> romantic comedy   science fiction film
> war film   western

Star Wars is a science fiction film.

2 Read the sentences. What types of film are the people talking about?

1
> The acting was great and I laughed from beginning to end!

2
> I couldn't look when Dracula came into her bedroom.

3
> My dad enjoyed it – but he's interested in history. I thought it was terrible.

4
> I cried at the end when he asked her to marry him.

5
> It was about American soldiers in Vietnam. I didn't really enjoy it. There was too much blood.

6
> The story was fantastic. I didn't want the film to finish. And the special effects were amazing. The aliens looked real!

7
> I enjoyed the film. The costumes were lovely, and the singing and dancing were great too.

3 Match each adjective with a film from exercise 2.

> boring   entertaining   funny   gripping   moving
> scary   violent

PART 2

Extension: *-ed* and *-ing* adjectives

4 Complete the table.

If a person or thing is …		then you are …	
	boring		bored
	annoying		annoyed
	1 _____		embarrassed
	exciting		2 _____
	3 _____		interested
	surprising		4 _____
	5 _____		confused
	disappointing		6 _____
	7 _____		frightened
	exhausting		8 _____

5 **SPEAKING** Describe the people in the photos. Use *-ed* adjectives from exercise 4.

> I think he looks …

> I don't think he looks …

 a
 b
 c
 d

6 **SPEAKING** Work in pairs. Use *-ing* adjectives to describe these things and experiences in your life.

1 a horror film
2 your English book
3 a shopping trip
4 the result of your last exam
5 a football match
6 an argument with a friend

> A horror film. It was frightening. It was also exciting.

7 Choose the correct adjectives.

1 I don't like this film. It's **bored / boring**.
2 This TV programme is very **interested / interesting**.
3 I love parties. They're really **excited / exciting**.
4 I forgot her name. It was really **embarrassed / embarrassing**.
5 I'm really **annoyed / annoying** because I can't find my mobile phone.
6 I'll be **surprised / surprising** if England win the World Cup.
7 It was an **exhausted / exhausting** tennis match, but I won in the end.
8 I worked hard last term, but my exam results were **disappointed / disappointing**.

VOCABULARY BUILDER ⑤

PART 1

1 Label the pictures with the words in the box.

| card shop | chemist's | clothes shop | electrical store |
| newsagent's | shoe shop | sports shop | supermarket |

 a

 b

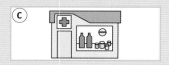 c

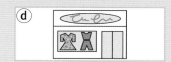 d

 e

 f

 g

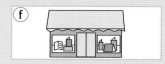 h

2 Where can you buy these things?

 ①

 ②

 ③

 ④

 ⑤

 ⑥

 ⑦

3 **SPEAKING** Memory Game! Take it in turns around the class to repeat the whole sentence adding your idea.

A I went to the **shoe shop** and bought **a pair of trainers**.

B I went to the shoe shop and bought a pair of trainers.
Then I went to **the supermarket** and bought **some bread**.

C I went to the shoe shop and bought a pair of trainers.
Then I went to the supermarket and bought some bread.
Then I went to **the card shop** and bought **a birthday card**.

PART 2

Extension: shopping and money

4 Complete the sentences with the correct form of the verbs from the box.

Verbs: shopping and money
borrow   buy   charge   cost   lend   owe
pay for   save   sell   spend

1 'Do you _____ birthday cakes?' 'No, we don't. Try the baker's down the road.'
2 I've run out of money. Can you _____ me some?' 'OK, how much do you want to _____?'
3 'They _____ me £500 for this computer.' 'That's expensive.'
4 Don't forget, you _____ me £50!
5 'I _____ these trainers at the sports shop in town.' 'Really? How much did they _____?'
6 Ben gets £10 pocket money. He usually _____ about half of it and _____ the rest for the future.
7 Can I _____ this CD with a credit card?

5 Complete the sentences so that both sentences mean the same. Use the verbs in brackets.

1 Can you lend me £5? (borrow)
Can _I borrow £5_?
2 I'd like to buy that DVD player, but I haven't got enough money. (afford)
I'd like to buy that DVD player _____.
3 I borrowed £10 from my dad. (lend)
My dad _____.
4 I paid £10 for my schoolbag. (cost)
My schoolbag _____.
5 You shouldn't spend that money. (save)
You _____.
6 I used a credit card to buy those CDs. (pay for)
I _____ with a credit card.
7 How much did that MP3 player cost? (charge)
How much _____ for that MP3 player?
8 My brother lent me £20. (owe)
I _____ £20.

6 Complete the sentences with the correct prepositions from the box. (In two sentences you don't need a preposition.)

| for | for | from | from | on | to |

1 If you need more money, borrow it _____ your parents.
2 Can you lend _____ me some money?
3 He spent £1,000 _____ a new TV.
4 Who's going to pay _____ the cinema tickets?
5 How much do I owe _____ you?
6 Burgers cost £2. They charge extra _____ cheese.
7 I bought this personal stereo _____ the electrical store in town.
8 I sold my old bike _____ my cousin.

VOCABULARY BUILDER 6

PART 1

1 Match the pictures with the descriptions.

 **a**

 **b**

 **c**

 **d**

 **e**

1 You listen to radio programmes on it.
2 You can take photographs without using a film.
3 You use it to watch films recorded on disc.
4 You use it to record video pictures of your friends, family, etc.
5 You use it to watch films recorded on cassette.

2 Complete the sentences with the words in the box.

| calculator | games console | mobile phone |
| MP3 player | satellite TV | stereo |

1 I love my new _____. It's really small, but it's got more than 5,000 songs on it!
2 I always use a _____ in maths lessons – unfortunately, we can't use them in exams.
3 I've got a _____ in my bedroom. It includes a radio, a CD player and a cassette deck.
4 We've got _____ at home. There's a choice of more than 100 TV channels!
5 I usually play computer games at my friend's house because he's got a new _____.
6 I've got a new _____. It's also a camera and an MP3 player!

PART 2

Phrasal verbs

3 Look at the pictures and phrasal verbs. Match the opposites.

 1 turn on / switch on

 a put away

 2 turn up

 b turn off / switch off

 3 take out

 c take off

 4 pick up

 d turn down

 5 put on

 e put down

4 Complete the sentences with the prepositions in the box.

| away | down | off | on | out | up |

1 When I switched _____ the light, the room was completely dark.
2 Can you turn _____ that music? It's too loud!
3 Can you pick _____ my calculator? I dropped it on the floor.
4 She took _____ her phone and made a call.
5 Please put _____ the DVDs when you've watched them.
6 Turn _____ the TV. It's time for my favourite programme.

5 Study the information in the *Learn this!* box. Rewrite the sentences using the object pronoun in brackets.

LEARN THIS!
When we use this type of phrasal verb with an object pronoun (*me*, *him*, *it*, *them*, etc.), we must put it between the verb and the preposition.
*Please turn up **the music**. Please turn **it** up.*

1 Can you switch off your mobile? (it)
2 He put down his books. (them)
3 He picked up his baby daughter. (her)
4 I put on my trainers. (them)
5 Turn on the lights! (them)
6 Take off that hat! (it)
7 Please put away your calculator. (it)
8 She put down the baby. (him)

VOCABULARY BUILDER 7

PART 1

1 Label the pictures with the words in the box.

> beckon   cross your legs   fold your arms   hold hands   nod
> point (at somebody/something)   shake your head   wink

a

b

c

d

e

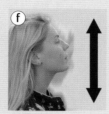
f

g

h

2 Complete the sentences using the words and phrases in the box.

> beckon   bow   hold hands   hug   nod
> pat you on the back   shake your head   wave

1 In most European countries, you _____ to mean 'no'.
2 In most European countries, you _____ to mean 'yes'.
3 You _____ somebody if you want them to come to you.
4 You often _____ to somebody when you say goodbye.
5 People sometimes _____ when they say 'well done'.
6 Couples sometimes _____ while they're walking.
7 You often _____ family members if you haven't seen them for a long time.
8 Many Asian people _____ to show respect when they meet somebody.

3 [SPEAKING] Work in pairs. Take turns to be A and B.
Student A: Choose a gesture from exercises 1 or 2. Do it or mime it.
Student B: Say what Student A is doing.

> You're patting somebody on the head.

PART 2

Phrasal verbs

4 Label the pictures with the phrasal verbs in the box.

> sit down   stand up   hold out your arms   turn over
> turn round   sit up   put up your hand   lift up your foot
> lie down   bend down

a

b

c

d

e

f

g

h

i

j

5 Choose the correct phrases.

1 When she saw me, she **held out her arms / put up her hand** and hugged me.
2 When the alarm clock rang, he **turned round / turned over** and went back to sleep.
3 Can you **lift up your foot / stand up**, please? You're standing on my toes!
4 He **bent down / lay down** and picked up some money from the floor.
5 I heard voices behind me, so I **bent down / turned round** and looked.
6 Please **lift up your foot / put up your hand** if you know the answer.
7 **Lie down / Stand up** on your bed if you're not feeling very well.
8 She came into the room and **sat up / sat down** on the chair.

VOCABULARY BUILDER 8

PART 1

1 Match the global issues from the box with the pictures.

> the arms trade   child labour   disease   endangered species
> famine   global warming   homelessness   pollution
> poverty   racism   terrorism   war

2 Which global issues are the newspaper headlines about?

ⓐ **Bomb explodes in London**

ⓑ **France sells fighter planes to Syria**

ⓒ **Asian man attacked by white youths**

ⓓ **100,000 people living on the streets in the UK**

ⓔ **US Forces invade Iraq**

ⓕ **New medicines could save millions of lives**

ⓖ **3 billion people live on less than $2 a day**

ⓗ **Renewable energy is the answer to climate change say scientists**

PART 2

Word formation: noun suffixes

3 Study the information in the *Learn this!* box. Find one noun in exercise 1 that ends in *-tion* and one that ends in *-ness*.

> **LEARN THIS!**
>
> We can form nouns by adding suffixes (word endings) to verbs or adjectives. Sometimes the spelling changes.
>
> 1 verb + *-ion*/*-ation*
>   discuss → discussion
>   organise → organisation
>
> 2 adjective + *-ness*
>   happy → happiness
>   dark → darkness

4 Complete the table. (The spelling changes in *one* of the nouns.)

Verb	Suffix	Noun
inform	-ation	1 _____
educate	-ation	2 _____
act	-ion	3 _____
suggest	-ion	4 _____
Adjective	**Suffix**	**Noun**
sad	-ness	5 _____
good	-ness	6 _____

5 🎧 2.28 **PRONUNCIATION** Listen and repeat. Underline the stress on the verbs, adjectives and nouns in the table above. When is the stress on the noun different from the stress on the verb or adjective?

6 Complete the sentences with nouns from exercise 4 and the *Learn this!* box.

1 Could you give me some i_____ about trains to London, please?
2 Fruit and vegetables are full of g_____.
3 'It's a very long film. Why don't we eat before we go to the cinema?' 'That's a very good s_____.'
4 They had a d_____ about global warming.
5 It's important that young people leave school with good qualifications. I think the government should spend more money on e_____.
6 The lights went out but our eyes quickly got used to the d_____.
7 My uncle works for Greenpeace. It's a large o_____ that campaigns for the environment.

VOCABULARY BUILDER ⑨

PART 1

1 Complete the crimes with the endings in the box.

-ary	-er	-ery	-ft	-ing	-ing	-ing	-ism

1 drug deal_____
2 joyrid_____
3 vandal_____
4 shoplift_____
5 robb_____
6 burgl_____
7 murd_____
8 the_____

2 Complete the sentences with the types of criminal in the box.

> burglar   drug dealer   joyrider   murderer   robber
> shoplifter   thief   vandal

1 If you murder someone, you are a _____.
2 If you steal things from shops, you are a _____.
3 If you sell drugs, you are a _____.
4 If you break into a house and steal things, you are a _____.
5 If you break things, for example, shop windows or telephone boxes, you are a _____.
6 If you steal cars and drive them round for fun, you are a _____.
7 If you steal money from somebody's bag, you are a _____.
8 If you steal a lot of money from a bank, you are a _____.

3 Match the crimes in exercise 1 with the types of criminal in exercise 2.

4 Complete the sentences with the correct form of the verbs in the box.

> go joyriding   rob   steal   burgle   spray   vandalise
> murder

1 Robin Hood _____ the rich and gave to the poor.
2 Somebody _____ my bicycle last week. I hope the police catch the thief.
3 Somebody _____ the bus shelter last night. They broke the glass and _____ graffiti.
4 A couple of teenagers _____ three houses in our street. They took money and jewellery.
5 Somebody _____ a drug dealer in Birmingham yesterday. They found his body in a park.
6 A boy and a girl _____ last night. They stole a car and crashed it into a street lamp.

PART 2

Word formation: noun suffixes -er, -ist and -ian

5 Study the information in the *Learn this!* box. Find five words with the *-er* suffix in the box in exercise 2.

> **LEARN THIS!**
>
> Words that describe a person who does a particular activity often end in *-er*, *-ist* or *-ian*.
>
> 1 Words that end *-er* are often connected with a verb:
>   *A writer is somebody who writes.*
>   *A teacher is somebody who teaches.*
>
> 2 Words that end *-ist* are often connected with a noun:
>   *A pianist plays the piano.*
>   *An artist makes works of art.*
>
> 3 Words that end *-ian* are often connected with an *-ical* adjective or a noun.
>   *A politician makes political decisions.*
>   *A magician does magic.*

6 Complete the words with the correct suffix: *-er*, *-ist* or *-ian*. Use the information in the *Learn this!* box to help you.

1 He's a music____. He plays music.
2 She's a build____. She builds houses.
3 He's a photograph____. He photographs famous people.
4 She's a guitar____. She plays the guitar.
5 He's a technic____. He does technical work in a laboratory.
6 She's a tour____. She's doing a tour of the USA.
7 He's a novel____. He writes novels.
8 She's a sing____. She sings.

7 Match the pictures (a–h) with the people in exercise 6 (1–8).

VOCABULARY BUILDER 10

PART 1

1 Label the pictures with words from the box.

atlas   autobiography   biography   comic   cookbook
dictionary   encyclopaedia   guidebook   magazine
manual   newspaper   novel   play   textbook

①

②

③

_____

④
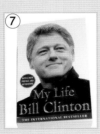
⑤

_____

⑥

⑦

_____

2 Complete the definitions with the other seven words from exercise 1.

1 A _____ is a book of instructions for a car or other device.
2 A _____ is a magazine of picture stories.
3 A _____ is a book that you use in lessons at school or college.
4 A _____ contains words and their definitions.
5 A _____ is a book that someone writes about someone else's life.
6 A _____ is a show that you see at the theatre.
7 An _____ contains information about lots of different subjects.

3 Write one real example of each type of publication (in English or in your language).

1 a play _____
2 a novel _____
3 a textbook _____
4 a magazine _____
5 a dictionary _____
6 a newspaper _____

PART 2

Books and text

4 Label the pictures with the words from the box.

back cover   chapter   contents page   front cover
hardback   paperback   spine   title

the b_____ c_____   the f_____ c_____

the s_____

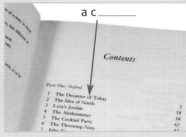

SUMMER ROMANCE

A SUMMER ROMANCE

Livinia Finnegan

the t_____

a h_____ book

a c_____

Contents

Part One: Oxford
1   The Decanter of Tokay
2   The Idea of North
3   Lyra's Jordan   3
4   The Alethiometer   18
5   The Cocktail Party   34
6   The Throwing-Nets   67

a p_____ book   the c_____ page

5 Draw lines to match the punctuation in the text with the descriptions.

THE FINAL COUNTDOWN
By Simon H Mancini

The noise of the engine was deafening. Jack Burtles knew that today would be like no other. After five years of training, the day had finally arrived – he was going into space.

'Ready for countdown,' instructed the first officer. 'Are all the systems functioning?'

Back in mission control, the countdown began.

'Stop! Stop!' a lone voice shouted. Jack felt his heart miss a beat as he sat confused and scared.

capital (upper case) letters

small (lower case) letters

full stop

comma

question mark

quotation marks

dash

exclamation mark

6 SPEAKING Work in pairs. Answer the questions about the book in exercise 5.

1 What is the title?
2 What is written on the spine?
3 How many capital letters are there on the front cover?
4 Are there any exclamation marks on the front or back cover?
5 How many question marks are there in this exercise?

OXFORD
UNIVERSITY PRESS

Great Clarendon Street, Oxford OX2 6DP

Oxford University Press is a department of the University of Oxford.
It furthers the University's objective of excellence in research, scholarship,
and education by publishing worldwide in

Oxford   New York

Auckland Cape Town Dar es Salaam Hong Kong Karachi
Kuala Lumpur Madrid Melbourne Mexico City Nairobi
New Delhi Shanghai Taipei Toronto

With offices in

Argentina Austria Brazil Chile Czech Republic France Greece
Guatemala Hungary Italy Japan Poland Portugal Singapore
South Korea Switzerland Thailand Turkey Ukraine Vietnam

OXFORD and OXFORD ENGLISH are registered trade marks of
Oxford University Press in the UK and in certain other countries

© Oxford University Press 2007

The moral rights of the author have been asserted

Database right Oxford University Press (maker)

First published 2007

2012 2011 2010 2009
10 9 8 7 6

ISBN: 978 0 19 455166 3   Student's Book
ISBN: 978 0 19 455167 0   MultiROM
ISBN: 978 0 19 455165 6   Pack

Printed in China

ACKNOWLEDGEMENTS

*The publisher and authors are very grateful to the many teachers and students who read and
piloted the manuscript, and provided invaluable feedback. With special thanks to:* Danica
Gondova, Martin; Kati Elekes, Budapest; Ferenc Kelemen, Budapest; Hana
Musílková, Prague; Zsuzsanna Nyirő, Budapest; Eva Paulerová, Pisek; Dagmar
Škorpíková, Prague.

The publisher and authors would like to extend their special thanks to: Ela Rudniak and
Małgorzata Wieruszewska, for the part they played in developing the material.

*The authors and publisher are grateful to those who have given permission to reproduce the
following extracts and adaptations of copyright material:* p9 'Sk8er Boi' Words & Music
by Lauren Christy, Scott Spock, Graham Edwards & Avril Lavigne © 2002
Warner/Chappell Music, Mr Spock Music, Holly Lodge Music, WB Music Corp,
Rainbow Fish Publishing and Almo Music Corporation. All rights on behalf of
itself, Mr Spock Music, Holly Lodge Music, Rainbow Fish Publishing & WB Music
Corp administered by Warner/Chappell Music Ltd, London W6 8BS. Reproduced
by permission of Warner Chappell and Hal Leonard Corporation; p13 'Talking
about your feelings' by Richard S Kingsley, December 2004 This information was
provided by KidsHealth, one of the largest resources online for medically
reviewed health information written for parents, kids and teens.
www.kidshealth.org © 1995–2007 The Nemours Foundation; p28 extracts from
'Introducing the Mayor of Monowi (population1)' by Tim Reid from *The Times* 19
February 2005 © News International Syndication 2005; p36 'Nobody Does It
Better' Words and Music by Carole Bayer Sager and Marvin Hamlisch © United
Artists Music Co Inc, Unart Music Corporation and EMI United Partnership Ltd,
USAWorldwide print rights controlled by Alfred Publishing Co Inc, USA.
Administered in Europe by Faber Music Ltd. Reproduced by permission. All
Rights Reserved; p77 'I Wish I Knew How It Would Feel To Be Free' words and
music by Billy Taylor and Dick Dallas © 1964 Duane Music Inc assigned to
Westminster Music. International Copyright Secured. All Rights Reserved. used
by permission; p98 extracts from an interview with Christopher Paolini on
www.teenreads.com © 2003 by Christopher Paolini. Reprinted with permission
of Alfred A Knopf Books for Young Readers. All Rights Reserved; p99 'Paperback

Writer' lyrics by John Lennon/Paul McCartney © Northern Songs/Sony ATV Music
Publishing. All Rights Reserved.

We would like to thank the following for their permission to reproduce photographs:
AA World Travel Photolibrary p27; Ancient Art and Architecture Picture Library
p97 (Bible); Alamy pp6 (soccer), 31 (beach), 33 (tidy room), 44 (jeweller), 47, 49 (St
Peters, The Kremlin), 56 (Ethan, Cindy); 70, 71, 73 (both), 77, 81 (immunisation),
83 (dancer), 95 (*The Big Issue*), 128 (chicken), 130 (pointing), 132 (technician,
bricklayer); Apple pp54 (ipod), 59 (laptop), 128 (laptop); Arnos Design pp12, 26
(road sign), 43, 53 (camera shop), 54 (TV, calculator, Walkman), 56 (text message),
59 (mini), 60, 63, 67 (mirror), 76 (plastic bag), 90, 94 (all), 95 (NY Times), 97
(Wikipedia), 100, 101, 103, 125 (rugby ball), 128 (jacket, necklace, stamps), 129
(DVD player), 130 (beckoning, shaking, nodding), 133 (novel, cookbook,
magazine, autobiography, paperback, contents page); Art Directors/TRIP p65
(Chinese meal); Brunswick Films Ltd p17 (car crash); Camera Press pp8 (hoodies),
16, 65 (Arabic food), 98; Canon p129 (camcorder); Capital Pictures p41; Casio p59
(*Baby-G* watch); Collections p26 (village); Corbis pp6 (watching tv), 10, 12, 14
(golf), 19, 20, 21, 26 (headshots), 38 (both), 39 (Hitchcock, Schwarzenegger), 42,
44 (CDs, butcher, baker), 46, 48 (Warsaw), 49 (Balmoral, Sydney), 50, 51, 55, 56
(Darren), 67 (magpie, Salamanca), 69, 74 (war), 84 (burglar), 96 (Shakespeare, The
Globe), 104, 120,125 (ice skates, basketball), 127 (annoyance, confusion), 130
(holding hands, winking, crossing legs), 132 (guitarist); Empics pp125 (male
runner, winning runner, woman playing soccer, tennis, losing man), 127
(surprise), 131 (disease, famine, global warming); European Youth Eco Parliament
p76 (logo); Fuji p54 (digital camera); Getty Images pp13, 14 (tennis, soccer), 15
(Moussambani, Pat Rafter), 17 (boat wreck), 32 (soccer), 33 (messy room), 53 (girl),
81 (girl), 85 (car), 93 (cafe), 96 (Andy, Sarah, Mike), 127 (embarrassed), 132
(violinist, singer, photographer, tourist, novelist); Kobal Collection pp4 (Trinity,
Blofeld, Garfield, Yoda), 34 (*Mission Impossible 3, Madagascar, The Day After Tomorrow,
Oliver, Chicago, Along Came Polly*), 35 (*The Aviator, Gladiator*), 36 (all), 37; London
Features International p9 (computer games); Masterfile p6 (computer games); Ron Morris/
2bangkok.com p68 (Thailand); Moviestore Collection p4 (Cruella de Vil); Nokia
p54 (mobile phone); OUP pp6 (swimming), 7 (all), 11 (all), 32 (cyclist), 40 (teens),
48 (Statue of Liberty), 49 (Pisa), 56 (Paula, girl texting), 57 (girl), 74 (panda), 75
(earth), 79 (volcano), 80, 106, 114, 125 (clubs, shuttlecock, hoop), 128 (bread, CD),
133 (guidebook); Panos Pictures p74 (poverty, child labour); Photofusion p84
(vandal); Popperfoto p15 (soccer); PURE p129 (digital radio); Delia and Kathy
Purviance p29 (Monowi today); PYMCA p8 (skinheads); Random House p99; Retna
p39 (Zeta-Jones), 57 (couple); Rex Features pp35 (Tom Hanks), 39 (Paltrow,
Kidman), 54 (games console), 68 (cheese rolling), 74 (homeless), 75 (Daryl
Hannah), 83 (drummer), 93 (prison), 122; Science Photo Library pp58, 59
(satellite, robot, CCTV), 74 (pollution), 76 (power station, crop sprayer), 84 (drug
dealer, shoplifter), 86, 92 (earthquake, fire), 125 (weights), 129 (video recorder),
131 (arms trade); Sony p54 (stereo); Still Pictures p92 (car in flood); Superstock
pp8 (punk), 66, 130 (folding arms); Topham Picturepoint p31 (York); TRH Pictures
p59 (nuclear weapon); Dan Tuffs p28 (Monowi 1950s), 29 (Elsie Eiler).

Illustrations by: Jonas Bergstrand/CIA pp16, 125, 126; Claude Bordeleau/Agent 002
pp5, 17, 55, 64, 77, 87, 111, 114, 118, 124; Paul Daviz p91; Jean-Luc Guerin/
Comillus pp24 (ex1, ex 4), 78, 79, 92, 95; Andy Lackow p25; David Oakley/Arnos
Design pp57 (truth and love machines), 116, 133 (atlas, hardback); Stephen
Strong pp40 (credit card, theatre), 88–89; Fred Van Deelen/The Organisation
pp14, 24 (ex 3), 30 (all), 128, 129, 130.

Cover Image: Corbis

Solutions Pre-Intermediate MultiROM

In your computer
- Interactive activities to practise the grammar and vocabulary in the Student's Book
- Exercises to help improve your writing and listening
- Games to help you revise what you've learned

In your CD player
- Audio tracks for listening exercises in Solutions Pre-Intermediate Workbook

1 Listening 1, page 20–21
2 Listening 2, page 38–39
3 Listening 3, page 48–49
4 Listening 4, page 58–59
5 Listening 5, page 68–69
6 Listening 6, page 78–79
7 Listening 7, page 88–89
8 Listening 8, page 98–99